JEANNETTE RANKIN

JEANNETTE RANKIN
Political Pioneer

Gretchen Woelfle

CALKINS CREEK

Honesdale, Pennsylvania

To Madeline Erskine, born in 1911,
when Jeannette worked for women's suffrage

Text copyright © 2007 by Gretchen Woelfle
All rights reserved
Printed in China
Designed by Helen Robinson
First edition

LIBRARY OF CONGRESS CATALOGING-IN-PUBLICATION DATA
Woelfle, Gretchen.
Jeannette Rankin : political pioneer / by Gretchen Woelfle.
p. cm.
Includes bibliographical references and index.
ISBN-13: 978-1-59078-437-2 (hardcover : alk. paper)
1. Rankin, Jeannette, 1880–1973—Juvenile literature.
2. Women legislators—United States—Biography—Juvenile literature.
3. Legislators—United States—Biography—Juvenile literature.
4. United States. Congress. House—Biography—Juvenile literature.
5. Social reformers—United States—Biography—Juvenile literature.
6. Feminists—United States—Biography—Juvenile literature. I. Title.
E748.R223W64 2006
328.73'092—dc22
[B]
2006012148

CALKINS CREEK
An Imprint of Boyds Mills Press, Inc.
A Highlights Company

815 Church Street
Honesdale, Pennsylvania 18431

ACKNOWLEDGMENTS

Books are collaborative ventures. I'd like to thank Carolyn P. Yoder, editor extraordinaire, for expecting more (and more!) of me all along the way. Professor Joan Hoff of Montana State University was kind enough to read the manuscript and offer suggestions both historical and literary. Researchers at the Montana Historical Society, the Mansfield Library at the University of Montana at Missoula, the Peace Collection at the Swarthmore College Library, and the Schlesinger Library at Harvard responded graciously to my many requests for information, documents, and photographs. The Ragdale Foundation offered me exquisite hospitality during a writer's residency. Thanks also to Sherrill Kushner, Alexis O'Neill, and Cleo Woelfle-Erskine, who read early drafts of the book, and Wendy Apple and Allyson Adams, who reminded me, once again, about Jeannette.

Contents

CHAPTER ONE: Still Marching   11

CHAPTER TWO: Growing Up in Montana   14

CHAPTER THREE: The Making of a Progressive   22

CHAPTER FOUR: Back Home to Montana   30

CHAPTER FIVE: The Road to Congress   40

CHAPTER SIX: "I Cannot Vote for War."   48

CHAPTER SEVEN: Fighting for Peace   58

CHAPTER EIGHT: Back to Congress   72

CHAPTER NINE: A Leader Once Again   80

Timeline   90

Selected Bibliography   93

Source Notes   95

Picture Sources   99

Index   101

JEANNETTE RANKIN

CHAPTER ONE

Still Marching

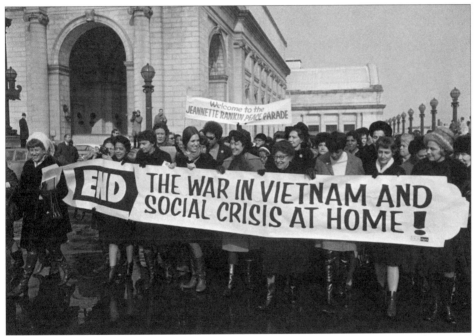

The marchers called themselves the Jeannette Rankin Brigade, but that was too militaristic for Jeannette. She preferred the name on the sign in the background that read Welcome to the Jeannette Rankin Peace Parade. Jeannette is the short woman wearing eyeglasses, in the middle of the front row.

O N JANUARY 15, 1968, FIVE THOUSAND WOMEN GATHERED AT the train station in Washington, D.C. They called themselves the Jeannette Rankin Brigade—not a military unit but an army of women dedicated to peace. Jeannette Rankin, eighty-seven years old, marched in the front row through the streets to the Capitol Building, where the U.S. Congress meets. Though she looked rather small and frail, she remained the feisty girl who wasn't afraid of an injured horse on her father's ranch in Montana. She was still the bold young woman who dared to stand on a soapbox on a street corner and explain why women should have the right to vote. She was the same Jeannette who wasn't afraid to speak her mind and vote against war in Congress. When someone asked her what made her so bold, she said, "I don't know. Just stubborn, I guess."

January 15, 1968, was a cold, gloomy day in Washington, D.C., and Congress was meeting for the first time in the new year. Jeannette had helped to gather these women from all across the United States to protest against the Vietnam War. The United States armed forces had been fighting in Vietnam for several years, and the war grew fiercer with each passing year.

Since 1954, Vietnam had been a divided country enveloped in a civil war. U.S. forces fought alongside the South Vietnamese Army against North Vietnam. Nearly twenty thousand American soldiers had died by 1968, and Jeannette Rankin wanted women to stand up and march to end the war.

The women—black, brown, white, young, middle-aged, and old—trudged through the snow for half a mile from the train station to the Capitol Building. Police lined the streets, ready to act against the marchers if they turned violent. But these women in black mourning clothes wanted peace. Theirs was a peaceful protest.

When the women came close to the Capitol, a young policeman walked up to Jeannette Rankin and took hold of her arm. Was he trying to help her? She *was* eighty-seven years old, after all. Was he trying to stop her? She shook him off and said, "You don't need to worry about us. We are unarmed and not at all threatening. Do you really need those great big guns to handle an old lady?" Then she climbed the stairs of the Capitol without any help.

The work of educating the world for peace is a woman's job, because men are afraid of being classed as cowards.
Jeannette Rankin, 1925

Over the years, Jeannette had lost none of her courage, none of her commitment, and none of her sense of humor. She had marched in parades and protests for sixty years. She also marched into Congress in 1917—as the first congresswoman—before most women even had the right to vote! She worked for peace even when people hated her for it, even when her friends told her she was wrong. When she wasn't marching with others, she stood alone.

> We haven't taken care of our children. We haven't educated our people. We haven't done the things necessary to make a happy nation.
>
> *Jeannette Rankin, 1972*

Jeannette Rankin came from a pioneer family. The same spirit of adventure and determination that sent her parents out West sent Jeannette into the world of politics, social reform, and nonviolence. This was difficult territory—especially for a woman. But this was the kind of adventure Jeannette Rankin loved. She was a political pioneer.

JEANNETTE RANKIN
HELENA, MONTANA

November 27, 1967

TO ALL AMERICAN WOMEN,

I am proud of the fact that my first vote cast in Congress was a vote against war. It was the first opportunity for a woman to vote because I was the first woman to be elected to Congress.

I believed then as I do today that women are the ones who must be concerned with the needs and development of the human race. I have always fought for the dignity of all human beings—for those of the present as well as those of future generations.

I will continue to struggle as long as I live.

I hope all women will respond to the following CALL, and join me in Washington on January 15, 1968, the opening day of Congress.

With highest hopes,

Jeannette Rankin

JEANNETTE RANKIN

Peace activists and feminists called on Jeannette to sponsor a women's protest march in Washington, D.C., in January 1968. Jeannette, eighty-seven years old, was happy to oblige.

CHAPTER TWO

Growing Up in Montana

Glaciers, forming and melting over more than thirty thousand years, carved out the broad Missoula Valley of Montana with its many rivers and streams. John Rankin built a ranch in the valley at Grant Creek. Jeannette spent a happy childhood there.

ONE SUMMER DAY, ON A RANCH NEAR MISSOULA, MONTANA, over one hundred years ago, a horse came galloping wildly across the plain to the farmyard. There was a wild look in its eyes, and the ranch hands soon discovered why. The horse had run into some barbed wire, and blood flowed from a nasty wound on its shoulder. Jeannette

Rankin, twelve years old, knew just what to do. She ran to the house for hot water, needle, and thread. When she returned, several men struggled to hold the horse on the ground. Jeannette knelt down, washed the wound, and sewed the torn flesh with a needle and thread. She wasn't a bit scared—of blood or a thrashing horse. She saw what needed to be done, and she did it.

When Jeannette was born in 1880, Montana was not yet a state. It was a territory with rugged mountains, rivers, and prairies, along with a few ranches, mines, and settlements hardly big enough to call towns. The U.S. Army was steadily conquering native Indian tribes and exiling them to reservations. The rough-and-ready days of fur trappers and gold miners were over. Cattle ranches were covering the land, and Missoula, which got itself a railroad in 1883, was becoming a center of business and trade. Jeannette spent her first six years on her father's ranch, six miles from Missoula. After that the family spent only summers at the ranch. She slept in a tent and rode horseback across the plains and into the canyons. In 1889 nine-year-old Jeannette celebrated along with everyone else when Montana became the forty-first state.

The Rankin family in the 1880s. Left to right: Wellington, Harriet, John, Olive, Jeannette, and Philena. Philena died at age eight.

Jeannette learned to work hard, too. It wasn't easy making a new life in the West. Men, women, and children worked side by side. Jeannette helped to cook, sew, and baby-sit for her five younger siblings—brother, Wellington, and sisters Harriet, Mary, Edna, and Grace—but she didn't much like it. Jeannette could be bossy and bad-tempered. On the one hand, she

During the winter, the Rankins lived in this elegant house in Missoula. In the background looms the mountain they called Jumbo.

wanted to run things her way, but on the other hand, she didn't want to run them at all! All the Rankin children were strong-minded, but Jeannette was more so. One day at a family outing her mother said to her father, "If you can take care of Jeannette, I can take care of the rest of the children."

Jeannette didn't shrink from hard work, though. Besides working at home, she sometimes cooked for the men at her father's lumber camp. She helped run her father's hotel in Missoula. When their dog, Shep, stepped into a steel trap, Jeannette amputated his mangled foot and sewed up his leg. Then she sewed him a little leather boot and harness to wear over his stump. When Shep chewed off the boot, Jeannette scolded him and put it on again. She knew what to do, and she made sure that Shep knew it, too. He wore that leather boot until he died many years later.

Jeannette Rankin got some of her courage, perseverance, and sense of adventure from her parents. Back then, people called this "pioneer spirit." Her mother, Olive Pickering, came from a family of English farmers who had settled in New England before the American Revolution. Olive had been a schoolteacher in New Hampshire, but she wanted adventure, so in 1878 she traveled to Montana with her uncle and her sister. Her sister soon fled back East, claiming that Montana was no place to raise children. Olive disagreed.

So did John Rankin, Jeannette's father. They both thought Montana was a fine place to raise a family. John, the son of poor Scottish immigrants in Canada, left school after third grade to become a carpenter's helper. In 1870 John, age twenty-nine and a trained carpenter, came to Montana on a riverboat. When it got stuck on a sandbar, he picked up his toolbox and started walking. When he finally reached Missoula, he began building—houses, hotels, the first bridge across the Missoula River, and the first church. He bought himself some land for a ranch, cut down trees, and built a sawmill to make lumber to build more buildings.

John Rankin wouldn't let his children near the dangerous machinery in the sawmill, so the children played on the logs in the millpond and in the piles of sawdust. But Jeannette crept close to the workers and watched how they ran the machines. When you are a bright, bold girl, you don't always follow the rules.

Every fall Jeannette and her family traveled six miles from the ranch to Missoula for the winter. "You could almost see where the glacier came through in the Ice Age. [Missoula] was this level place. And then the mountains went up on each side everywhere. ... Back of our house was a great big grass-covered mountain fifteen hundred feet above the town and it looked just like an elephant. We always called it Jumbo."

In Missoula the Rankins lived in a three-story brick house. They had the first central heating in town, hot and cold running water, and a tub in the bathroom—luxuries in the mid-1880s. But Missoula meant school, and school meant sitting at a desk all day long, reciting out loud with the whole class, learning things that bored Jeannette. "I was a very poor student and I didn't enjoy going to school," she said.

Jeannette learned much more around the family dinner table. She and her mother cooked for the family and their many guests, making homemade cakes and ice cream for dessert. When Jeannette's father was in a jolly mood, he danced a Scottish jig. At other times, he was right in the middle of fierce arguments about politics and the future of Montana. The children had arguments, too, sometimes throwing things across the table, and one or another child stomping away.

One topic that infuriated John Rankin was the U.S. Army's treatment of the Indians. The army's policy was to drive the Indians off their lands with threats of violence. When Indian hunting grounds were seized by white settlers, the tribes were forced onto reservations, often far from their homelands. Chief Joseph and the Nez Perce Indians had been evicted from a reservation in Idaho and began a seventeen-hundred-mile march to Canada through Montana. They never made it. John Rankin told his children about the massacre of the Nez Perce braves and the surrender of Chief Joseph in 1877. Jeannette's father hated this cruel treatment. Guns and warfare were no way to settle anything, he argued. They only

The Salish Indians left their reservation north of Missoula every spring and traveled south of the town to harvest and hunt.

brought more violence. He didn't even allow any guns on his ranch. His opinion made sense to Jeannette—for the rest of her life.

The Rankin children often saw Salish Indians pass by their house on their way to the Missoula Valley south of town. There the Salish harvested bitterroot for food and medicine. They fished and hunted deer and elk, since the buffalo were gone. Jeannette and her siblings attended Indian celebrations. They listened to the drumming and singing and even learned some of the dances. Jeannette often told a favorite story that described how one white woman greeted a troop of Indians—peacefully.

When I was in school there was a boy that we always pointed out and talked about because when he was a tiny baby, he had a very unusual experience. His mother and father were crossing the plains in a covered wagon with a group of others. One day, when they were parked, they heard the Indians coming. All the men ran to the wagons to get their guns, and this little boy's mother ran to the wagon to get her tiny baby. ...

When [the Indians] came she handed them this tiny baby. ... It was the first time they'd ever seen a white baby, probably. They passed it around and talked. She couldn't understand what they said, and they couldn't understand whether she said, "We're not going to hurt you." But they could understand that that tiny baby was the most precious thing that she had, and that if she handed it to them, she trusted them. They handed the baby back and went away.

Jeannette told this story all her life. For her, it showed that trust and friendship, not threats and guns, were the ways to live together. Peaceful coexistence with the Indians made perfect sense to her, as well as to her father.

John Rankin admired Jeannette's intelligence and good sense. Once he bought a new machine to gather hay. As he drove a team of horses to pull the machine, it got stuck. He couldn't leave the horses to

By 1895, the Rankin family was complete. Back row, left to right: John, Jeannette, Harriet (standing), Wellington, and Olive. Seated in front, left to right: Mary, Edna, and Grace. The photograph is in memory of Philena.

look at the problem, but Jeannette saw what could be done. She told her father and he told the men how to fix it. Then he said to the men, "You haven't sense enough to do it yourself. You have to let a little girl tell you what to do." Jeannette was her father's idea girl. He turned to her to discuss new projects.

Jeannette (third player from the left) played basketball in high school until she broke her nose during one rambunctious game. Girls wore "bloomers," wide trousers that uncovered their lower legs, while playing sports. But they wore ankle-length skirts at all other times.

In high school Jeannette went to parties and dances. She played basketball in bloomers—loose pants—until she broke her nose. One weekend she invited some friends to the ranch for a picnic. Her father wasn't around, so

Jeannette (far right) and her friends formed a club called The Buds. In May 1902 they gave a ball for two hundred guests. It was the grandest social event of the year. But Jeannette was restless. In her diary she wrote, "Go! Go! Remember at the first opportunity go."

Jeannette in the science lab at the new Montana State University in Missoula. She majored in biology and wrote her senior thesis on snails found in the nearby mountains.

Jeannette's 1902 college graduation class. She is standing in the middle row, second from the left. Notice that there are more women than men.

she showed them how the sawmill worked. She assigned jobs to each of them and operated the heavy machinery herself. She was a take-charge sort of person.

In 1898 Jeannette entered the first freshman class of Montana State University, mostly because "it was just the thing to do and there didn't seem to be anything else." She wrote her senior thesis on snails and graduated with a degree in biology. She was usually quiet in class, but one day a professor asked her to read from Alfred, Lord Tennyson's famous war poem "The Charge of the Light Brigade."

> *Half a league, half a league,*
> *Half a league onward,*
> *All in the valley of Death*
> *Rode the six hundred.*
> *"Forward, the Light Brigade!*
> *"Charge for the guns!" he said:*
> *Into the valley of Death*
> *Rode the six hundred.*
> . … … … … . .
>
> *Their's not to make reply,*
> *Their's not to reason why,*
> *Their's but to do and die:*
> *Into the valley of Death*
> *Rode the six hundred.*

"This is hideous," Jeannette declared. "I can't read it." She was beginning to speak up for what she believed—and it wasn't the glory of war.

Jeannette went out with several young men and received more than one proposal of marriage, but refused them all. She didn't plan to spend her life keeping house and raising children. She had done enough of that! But if she didn't marry, what could a young woman do in 1902?

Jeannette liked running things. If she had been a boy, she probably would have taken over her father's work—ranching, building, buying property, serving as county commissioner. But this was men's work, not right for young women. Missoula wasn't a frontier settlement anymore. It had a railroad, a growing university, and four-story granite hotels and banks, one with a copper-covered dome. Respectable women married or became schoolteachers. Jeannette tried schoolteaching as her mother had done, but she didn't like teaching any more than she had liked

Missoula grew quickly at the end of the nineteenth century. By 1900 there were 4,356 residents and a horse-drawn trolley system. But the streets weren't paved yet. Women's long skirts dragged in the mud.

going to school. She worked as a seamstress, but *that* bored a young woman who thought for herself.

When John Rankin died in 1904, Olive Rankin retreated from household responsibilities and relied even more on Jeannette. Her youngest sisters, Edna and Grace, were twelve and eleven, no longer babies. But they still needed Jeannette to sew their clothes, bake their bread, and call the doctor to come and remove Edna's tonsils. The younger girls were afraid of Jeannette's quick temper and didn't dare complain when the dresses or the doctor weren't to their liking. Jeannette wasn't happy, either. All this housework and mothering didn't satisfy her.

What could she do with the rest of her life? Where could she find challenge and adventure?

CHAPTER THREE

The Making of a Progressive

Jeannette traveled to Washington, D.C., in 1905 to watch the inauguration of President Theodore Roosevelt and dance at the Inaugural Ball.

WHEN JEANNETTE'S BROTHER, WELLINGTON, WENT TO HARVARD College in Massachusetts, she managed to get time off from her housekeeping duties and crossed the country by train to visit him. She had never been East before. Wellington and her cousins arranged dates and parties for twenty-four-year-old Jeannette while she was in Boston. She traveled to New York City and even to Washington, D.C., to dance at the 1905 Inaugural Ball of President Theodore Roosevelt. Jeannette saw how wealthy people lived in grand mansions and dressed in elegant fashions.

Hungry men stand in line in New York City to receive a free meal. Jeannette saw such sights when she first visited Boston and New York in 1904–1905.

But in Boston and New York, she also saw shabby, unhealthy slums where hordes of people lived crowded together. Hungry, ragged children. People out of work or working for wages that couldn't feed their families. In Montana people weren't rich, but they weren't so dreadfully poor, either. Back home people had homes, jobs, and enough to eat. Jeannette began to read about the hard lives of city people. One 1905 book, *The Long Day: The Story of a New York Working Girl as Told by Herself,* remained in her library all her life. Back in Montana, still looking for something to do, Jeannette grew depressed and suffered from rheumatism. She boarded the train for San Francisco, hoping to find a healthier climate. She found more than that—a new direction for her life.

In the late nineteenth century, a Progressive reform movement arose to address problems caused by the rapid growth of industry and cities. Factory jobs lured people from farms and small towns into big cities. The promise of a good life brought millions of immigrants to the United States. But miserable living and working conditions awaited many of these people. They lived in unhealthy housing and worked in dangerous jobs. A few businessmen grew enormously rich while the workers remained poor.

Progressive reformers—both men and women—worked to improve people's lives in many ways. They established social services and education classes in neighborhood community centers, called settlement houses. They supported the rights of workers to form labor unions and go on strike. They tried to convince lawmakers to pass laws to improve health standards, housing, wages, and working conditions. And they entered politics themselves to make all this happen. Of all the Progressive

Jane Addams inspired Jeannette Rankin throughout her life. Addams founded Hull House, a large settlement house in Chicago. She was a prominent leader of women's suffrage and the peace movement. In 1931 she won the Nobel Peace Prize.

Jane Addams's Hull House in Chicago offered child care, health care, and recreational activities for immigrant children. It also offered English classes and job training for their parents.

reformers Jeannette Rankin read about, she admired Jane Addams most.

Addams had started Hull House in Chicago, a settlement house where poor immigrants could go for classes and advice. There were children's programs, too, run by social workers.

When Jeannette reached San Francisco, she visited the Telegraph Hill Neighborhood Association, a settlement house in an Italian neighborhood. She offered to help for a few days and stayed four months. She took care of the children while their mothers studied English, government, and health. She attended meetings about changing factory conditions and child labor laws. Finally she knew what to do with her life. She would become a social worker.

But first she had to learn more about such things, so she set out for New York City, a center for the new field of social work. Until around 1900 much of the "social work," such as Jeannette had done in San Francisco, was considered a volunteer hobby for middle-class women. Then attitudes started to change. Researchers began to keep records of the work of settlement houses and other institutions. They wrote books and journal articles. In 1904 the New York School of Philanthropy offered the first formal course of study in social work that led to a college degree. Social work became a respected profession. The school later became the Columbia University School of Social Work, which still exists today.

Jeannette enrolled in the New York School of Philanthropy in 1908. In the morning she attended classes in social reform, charity organization, social and racial progress, labor problems, and criminal sociology. In the afternoon she worked with poor people in their neighborhoods. At last she was excited about school. She studied harder than ever before and earned two A's and eight B's at the end of her first year.

Jeannette worked with poor children such as these when she studied social work at the New York School of Philanthropy.

During one school term, she worked with deaf children. A little boy's father had abandoned the family, and the mother, unable to care for her three small children, sent her deaf son to an orphanage. Jeannette was heartbroken. If she had had a proper home in New York, as she did in Montana, she said she would have adopted the boy herself.

Jeannette also worked at the night police court, trying to help young prostitutes obtain housing, medical care, and jobs. When Jeannette walked the dangerous streets of New York, she carried a billy club

Jeannette's 1909 graduating class at the New York School of Philanthropy had more women than men. Jeannette sits in the middle of the second row, without a fancy hat. She wears a complicated hairdo instead.

in a velvet bag, looking like a perfect lady, but fully prepared to defend herself. She was a woman now, living in the city, but she brought her girlhood bravery with her from Montana.

After Jeannette graduated in 1909, she returned to Montana. Her sisters Harriet and Mary had graduated from Montana State University, as her younger sisters, Grace and Edna, would. Wellington was at Harvard Law School. They didn't need Jeannette to take care of them anymore.

Missoula's downtown, around 1905, boasted multistoried department stores and hotels, some with towers and domes. It didn't seem to need the reform movement that Jeannette wanted to establish.

Large decorated hats were the fashion when Jeannette was a young woman. Here she sports one with ribbons and feathers.

She arrived in Missoula, ready to begin her career as a Progressive reformer, but she found no Progressive movement in Missoula, so she tried to start one. She raised some money to build a public bathhouse for miners who came into town, dirty from their rough life in the mountains. But the miners preferred to wash up in the saloons, so Jeannette had to give all the money back.

She saw that the jail was overcrowded, and men and women shared the same cells. So she started a campaign to improve conditions. Jeannette discovered that the deputy's family was living in half the jail building. No wonder the prisoners were so crowded! First she complained to the county attorney. "That's just Jeannette Rankin—it's nothing," he told the local judge. But Jeannette had roused her friends to action, and the judge replied, "Then why are all the good women in town telephoning me?" The deputy's family moved out and the prisoners had more room.

Jeannette couldn't find much to reform in Missoula, and she grew more restless than ever. She had lived in New York. She had seen poverty there but also social change that thrilled her. Missoula seemed so far from all that excitement. Determined to be a social worker, Jeannette found a job in an orphanage in Spokane, Washington. Soon she learned that her caring and hard work weren't enough. She said,

There wasn't enough money. There were too many children; only a few could be placed [in foster families]. Half of them returned when

people changed their minds. [The children] had suffered so much from poverty, were in such ill health, had such bad habits, that nobody wanted them. They came back and wept in my office. All those awfully sad things about the children—I couldn't take it.

Jeannette realized that social work would not change the system that created this terrible situation in the first place. But what could she do about it?

She looked for answers at the University of Washington in Seattle, where she studied economics, sociology, and public speaking. She got an H for honors in public speaking. Little did her professor know that his honors student would give more than six thousand speeches over the next sixty years, and that her voice would reach millions of people.

One day in Seattle Jeannette saw a poster asking for volunteers for the women's suffrage movement. The U.S. Constitution didn't give women suffrage—the right to vote—and some women had been trying to get that right for more than sixty years. Several western states and territories had granted suffrage to women, and women were struggling to gain it in other states. Of course, only men could vote to allow women to vote.

Jeannette didn't know much about women's suffrage. That was about to change. The day Jeannette walked into the Seattle suffrage office, she was handed a stack of posters to put up. She did the job and returned.

I was always taught that there was a brilliant period at the time of the Revolution, but I think that the first twenty years of [the twentieth] century had many brilliant people, especially women.
Jeannette Rankin

Like these volunteers in Washington State in 1910, Jeannette put up posters declaring that Women Should Vote.

At first I thought the word "men" in "all men are created equal" meant "people" and that women need only ask for the vote to get it. This wasn't true: we had to ask, insist, work, persist.
Jeannette Rankin

This flyer offers political and economic arguments to the men of Washington State to vote in favor of women's suffrage. Supporters listed in small print include Jane Addams and former president Theodore Roosevelt.

The women were surprised to see her back so soon. Where had she put them? On fences and light posts, in store windows and a barbershop. A barbershop! Jeannette Rankin had invaded exclusive male territory. Here was the kind of woman they needed. As for Jeannette, she watched the barber from across the street and reported that "the poster in his window brought him in a lot of jolly customers." They probably laughed at the idea of women voters, but at least they talked about the issue.

Washington State would soon be holding a general election to vote on women's suffrage, so Jeannette went to work. At first she gave speeches around the state accompanied by more experienced campaigners. Because she learned quickly, she soon traveled on her own. In some towns, "the only place we could talk was on the street!" Jeannette said. "We couldn't even get a hall." Wherever she went, Jeannette spoke her mind.

She told the women, "Your [state government] representative is a fine man, honest and independent. The only thing wrong with him is, he's against woman suffrage, and that's your fault. You haven't told him how you feel."

She told the men, "You men of the West are not afraid of your women, and you're not afraid to give them the vote."

To mixed audiences she insisted,

> *It's a woman's place to make a home, but she can't make it if she has no say in community conditions. It's beautiful and right that a woman should nurse her sick children through typhoid fever, but it's also beautiful and right that she should vote for sanitary measures to prevent that typhoid from spreading.*

Washington State men did what the suffragists wanted and granted women the right to vote in November 1910.

Here was the cause Jeannette Rankin had been looking for! Here was a cause that could use her intelligence, stubbornness, and hard work. Here was a cause that would truly make a difference in people's lives. Jeannette was hooked on women's suffrage.

A suffrage cartoon comically turns the tables on men. Here is a husband, stuck at home, while mother is working as a "suffragette."

Suffragists used humor as well as logic to get their message across. Notice that even respectable hens wore fancy hats.

CHAPTER FOUR

Back Home to Montana

The Montana state capitol was filled with a large crowd on February 1, 1911, to hear Jeannette speak to the state legislature, asking them to vote for women's suffrage. Right: Jeannette, thirty years old in 1911, worked full-time for women's suffrage. She traveled all around the United States, living out of suitcases, speaking and organizing suffrage campaigns. Jeannette dressed formally in those days, still wearing a big hat.

ON FEBRUARY 1, 1911, THE UPSTAIRS GALLERY OF THE STATE capitol in Missoula, Montana, was packed with visitors. Jeannette Rankin was about to give a speech—the first time a woman had spoken there to the men who made the laws for the state. Those men were going to decide whether to hold a general election on women's suffrage in Montana.

Flowers decorated the hall in Jeannette's honor. The men forbade smoking and removed all the spittoons, so no one could chew tobacco and spit that day. Jeannette's family—all suffragists—and others watched from the gallery. They worried that the lawmakers would jeer Jeannette as men often jeered the suffragists. There was no need for concern. Jeannette was brilliant.

She began by proclaiming, "I was born in Montana!" Wild applause broke out. Most Montanans had been born in other states or countries. They had settled in Montana with the same hope of a prosperous future that had brought John Rankin from Canada. But Jeannette claimed Montana as her own. Her roots were in the plains and mountains and the growing town of Missoula.

Jeannette talked about how Montana women had worked right alongside the men on farms and ranches. Women worked, they paid taxes, and they deserved the right to vote. She knew that the politicians worried about getting reelected. Would voters turn against them if they approved the cause of women's suffrage? Jeannette understood their concern, so she ended by saying, "We are not asking you gentlemen to decide this great question. We are merely asking you to leave it to the voters."

This photograph is a bit of a mystery. We can identify the setting as the porch of the Rankin house in Missoula. The women, old and young, gather around Jeannette, who sits on the steps. Many are wearing white buttons, too small to read. Written in the bottom right-hand corner of the photo is "R.H. McKay 1912." This identifies the photographer and, presumably, the date he took the photo. We can make an educated guess that these women are working for Montana suffrage, meeting at Jeannette's house, and advertising their political opinions on their lapels.

Applause was long and loud. Newspapers reported her speech all across the state. The *Helena Independent* wrote, "To Miss Jeannette Rankin … belongs the glory. … [She] spoke simply and with an earnestness that was both convincing and proof positive of the sincerity of her convictions. Her argument was sound as a dollar." She even changed some lawmakers' minds. When they voted on the women's suffrage bill, it gained over half the votes, but not the two-thirds majority it needed to pass. Jeannette still had work to do.

The heart of the national suffrage movement was in New York City, so Jeannette moved there to continue her work. Until that time, she had worked without pay. She had inherited some money when her father died in 1904 and received an income of $75 a month from that money—the wages of a Montana coal miner. She could afford to live on that in the family home in Missoula, but in New York she needed a salary. The New York Women's Suffrage Party, a state group, paid her $50 a month to work for votes for women in New York State. A year later she got a raise, to $125 a month.

Jeannette, always well dressed and charming, would stand on a street corner and ask a couple of people to wait just a moment. Then she gathered a few more. Finally, she climbed on a wooden soapbox to explain why women should have the vote and why men should give it to them. She even told children to ask their fathers why they wouldn't let their mothers vote.

In New York Jeannette met other women like herself—intelligent, energetic, and committed to reform. They formed a weekly club in Greenwich Village called Heterodoxy, which means disagreeing with accepted beliefs. The women talked and argued about books and politics and the best ways to change the world. They were New Women who questioned the old limitations men had placed on women's rights and roles in society. They believed that women should enter the worlds of business, law, and politics that men ruled. Women could marry or live with other women or live alone. Keeping a house and raising children was not the only path to a satisfying life. These Heterodoxy lunches in New York resembled the Rankin dinner table in Montana, with one difference—her father and his male friends didn't dominate the conversation. Men weren't even invited!

Jeannette worked for various local, state, and national suffrage groups for four years, crisscrossing the country from New York to California, making speeches and organizing local suffrage committees. She spoke to congressmen and to the state legislatures. She worked in fifteen states and Washington, D.C. It wasn't all hard work. Suffragists published newsletters filled with witty cartoons as well as hard facts. They held teas, luncheons, dinners, card parties, and dances—adding a dash of voting talk to every event.

The women succeeded little by little. Women could vote in a few states—all in the West. The National American Woman Suffrage Association (NAWSA), based in New York, wanted Congress to pass an amendment to the Constitution that would give the vote to women in the whole country. But Congress wasn't ready for that, so the campaigns continued state by state.

More and more people stood up for women's suffrage. But many men and women weren't convinced yet. Francis Parkman, a famous historian, wrote, "The female vote … is always more impulsive and less subject to reason, and almost devoid of the sense of responsibility." Some women believed they weren't intelligent enough or strong enough to think about, let alone take part in, politics. Jeannette Gilder, a prominent journalist, wrote an article called "Why I Am Opposed to Woman Suffrage." She stated, "In politics I do not think that women have any place. The life is too public, too wearing, and too unfitted to the nature of women."

Eleanor Roosevelt, who later became the most politically active First Lady the United States had ever seen, wasn't a suffragist at first. She wrote, "I took it for granted that men were superior creatures and knew more about politics than women." She, like most women, left such matters to her husband. When her husband, Franklin, finally became a suffragist, she decided "I probably must be, too."

In March 1913 President Woodrow Wilson took office and the suffragists planned a parade. Radio and television didn't exist, and parades were a good way to

When Woodrow Wilson was elected president of the United States in 1912, he opposed women's suffrage. It took six more years of speeches, marches, protests, arrests, and prison sentences before Wilson changed his mind and urged Congress to pass a constitutional amendment to give women the right to vote.

Suffragists organized a massive parade of five thousand marchers on the day before Wilson's inauguration. They wanted to proclaim their demand for equal political rights to all the visitors that had come to Washington, D.C.

The suffrage parade on March 3, 1913, began well, led by women on horseback. Then came women marching, riding on floats, and performing in bands. The Capitol, home of the U.S. Congress that could give them the vote, stood behind them.

During the parade, men mobbed the marchers, shouting insults, pushing, pinching, and spitting on the women, and tearing off their badges and banners. Here the crowd surrounds a float and stops the parade. The police did nothing to stop the riot. Order was finally restored by National Guard troops, Boy Scouts, and male college students.

reach the crowds that came to Washington, D.C., for the inauguration. Five thousand women gathered to march with banners, floats, and an all-woman band. Women from each state marched behind their flags. Jeannette Rankin led the Montana group, and her sister Edna, on her way to becoming a lawyer, marched beside her.

For decades, many men had ignored or laughed at the women suffragists. Now, seeing how strong the movement had become, some spectators became angry and violent. Men yelled insults at the marchers, threw lighted cigar butts, spat on them, and even knocked them down. Police stood by and did nothing. But the women kept marching, and finally army troops arrived to restore order. The next day the whole country read newspaper stories of the men's disgraceful actions, and suffragists won more people to their cause.

In 1913 the Montana legislature finally passed a bill to hold an election on women's suffrage. Montana men were going to vote on the issue in November 1914. In January 1914 Jeannette returned home and threw herself into the campaign.

She traveled thousands of miles across her huge state. She spoke at respectable tea parties and outside saloons. She visited farmers in their fields and lawmakers in the state capital. She gave speeches at town halls and factory gates, union meetings and courthouses, movie theaters and dance halls. Jeannette knew the campaign must go on after she left town, so she helped organize local suffrage groups to carry on the work.

State and county fairs drew large crowds of Montana's far-flung rural citizens. Jeannette and her suffragist friends were there with decorated stalls, banners, and booklets. Jeannette met with the leaders of all four political parties—Republican, Democrat, Progressive, and Socialist—and asked for their support. She got it. She wrote a letter to every registered voter in the state saying, "Women in our organization are from all walks of life, every political party, and every religion and faith. We unite on one point: we want to vote."

This broad-based appeal finally brought success to the women's suffrage campaigns in the West. From 1896–1910, despite much hard work, many suffrage campaigns failed, even in western states. The movement had attracted mostly middle-class women and men. Only when suffragists formed alliances with working-class men and women, often represented by the Progressive and Socialist political parties, did women win the vote for women in more states. In the East, only New York State learned this lesson, when the women won the vote in 1917. The rest of the eastern states had to wait for a

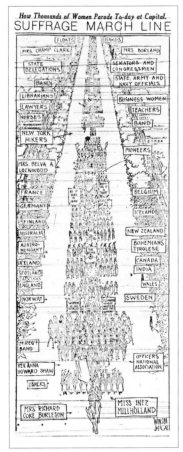

Women formed groups by nation, profession, state, political parties, clubs, and religion. Jeannette and her sister Edna marched with others from the state of Montana.

Carrie Chapman Catt (1859–1947) was a tireless leader for the cause of women's suffrage. Her stubborn, often dictatorial personality seemed to meet its match in Jeannette Rankin.

STOP LOOK LISTEN

Provided you are a live one. If dead already, stay where you are and be run over by the Suffragette Express that will overtake the fast male at the Missoula Theatre.

Miss Jeannette Rankin of the greatest city on earth will act as an engineer. ... Have your life insured and bring your firearms for there are going to be many bombs exploded and many balloons punctured.

Messages printed on posters in Missoula during the Montana women's suffrage campaign of 1914

constitutional amendment.

Jeannette loved traveling and speaking and speaking and organizing—and she was good at it. She became the national field secretary of the National American Woman Suffrage Association in 1913. But she had problems with Carrie Chapman Catt and other suffragist leaders in New York. Eastern women ran NAWSA, even though western women had achieved the vote. Wealthy women, who worked as volunteers, made decisions for workers like Jeannette, who earned a salary. Jeannette and other western women wanted more authority to organize their own activities. Jeannette always had a problem taking orders. She wanted to be in charge of her own work. She also grew impatient with suffragists who didn't work as hard as she did.

One night at the suffragist office in Butte, Montana, overworked and exhausted, Jeannette lost her temper and began shouting and throwing things. An old friend of hers calmed her down and later wrote to her about her outburst.

Never mind if you do not convert the multitude—others will follow after you who can complete the job. ... I appreciate what you are and feel that I must help protect you against yourself in the

VOTES FOR WOMEN.

For the work of a day,
For the taxes we pay,
For the Laws we obey,
We want something to say.

6542

Though this is a cartoon, the daughters of suffragists probably spoke to their young male friends this way.

Toasts

Toast Mistress . . . Miss Mary Stewart
"Special Privilege" .
. . Mr. Washington Jay McCormick
"The Men" . . Mrs. Tylar B. Thompson
"When Women Vote" . . Mr. Fred Angevine
"What Now?" . . Mr. A. L. Stone
"Votes For Women" . Miss Jeanette Rankin

BANQUET *in honor of* MISS JEANETTE RANKIN *to celebrate the* VICTORY OF EQUAL SUFFRAGE *in the* THIRTEENTH GENERAL ASSEMBLY OF MONTANA, *at* MISSOULA, FEBRUARY FIRST, NINETEEN HUNDRED THIRTEEN

"Votes for Women".

Menu

Sweet Pickles

Clear Consomme

Roast Young Montana Turkey
Chestnut Dressing

Cranberry Sauce

Mashed Potatoes

Potato Salad

Coffee

Ice Cream   Cake

Suffragists combined business with pleasure. Honored at a banquet in Missoula, her hometown, Jeannette enjoyed a fine dinner before giving the main speech of the day.

intense and even reckless passion to turn the world over like a flap-jack. ... Here in Butte we are all ready to kowtow before you—that is everyone but me—for once in a while I want to spank you good and hard. Now, will you be good?

One politician saw only her good side, and that was very good indeed. Montana Congressman Tom Stout, describing her success with various political groups, said,

> Jeannette Rankin is one of the most successful campaigners that I ever knew. I have seen her go into a Democratic Convention ... and secure an endorsement. Then she went into the Republican Convention where the opposition was stronger and won there.

She achieved all this by the charm of her manner and the force of her arguments.

Most of the time, Jeannette kept a firm hold on her hot temper, even when she was taunted with insults and bad jokes. When a political boss, snickering about women's suffrage, threw a glass of water in her face, she firmly promised that Montana women would vote him out of office.

In the fall, just before the Montana election, Jeannette and two other suffragist leaders led a mile-long parade at the state fair. Behind them marched horseback riders, brass bands, floats, groups of women and men, and even children with hat bands announcing "I want my mother to vote."

When the ballots were counted in November, Montana women had won. They could vote. After years of hard work, Jeannette was on the winning side at last.

On November 2, 1914, the day before the Montana election, suffragists continue to campaign. They, along with Jeannette, celebrated the next day when the women of Montana won the right to vote.

Women's Suffrage Timeline

Women received the right to vote little by little. For example, Sweden gave unmarried women the right to vote in local elections in 1862. All women there didn't receive full voting rights until 1921. In 1883 widows gained the vote in Canada. The rest of the women got the vote in 1918, except in Quebec, where women couldn't vote in provincial elections until 1940. Sometimes women were allowed to vote in local elections but not in national elections. In the United Kingdom women over the age of thirty got the vote in 1918. At the time, all men could vote at age twenty-one. Equal voting rights were finally granted to women in 1928. This timeline shows when countries granted all women the right to vote on equal terms with men.

1893	New Zealand
1906	Finland
1913	Norway
1915	Denmark
1918	Austria, Germany, Latvia, Poland, Russia
1919	The Netherlands, Ukraine
1920	United States, Czechoslovakia
1921	Armenia, Sweden
1928	Ireland, United Kingdom
1930	Turkey
1931	Spain, Ceylon
1932	Brazil, Thailand
1934	Cuba
1937	The Philippines
1942	Dominican Republic
1944	France
1945	Indonesia, Italy
1946	Vietnam
1947	Mexico
1948	Belgium, Israel
1949	China
1950	India
1952	Greece
1954	Colombia, Ghana
1955	Cambodia, Ethiopia, Honduras, Nicaragua, Peru
1956	Egypt
1963	Afghanistan, Congo, Iran
1971	Switzerland
1994	South Africa

CHAPTER FIVE

The Road to Congress

Auckland, New Zealand. Jeannette spent a year in New Zealand, working as a seamstress and learning about working conditions for women, who had received voting rights in 1893. She found it a "delightful, restful country."

A FTER THE SUCCESSFUL MONTANA SUFFRAGE CAMPAIGN, JEAN-nette took a break. Her spirit of adventure took her to New Zealand, where women had been voting since 1893. In addition to woman suffrage, the Liberal Party in that country had passed laws regulating industrial safety and granting workers the right to organize unions. Jeannette visited health clinics for women and children, attended labor union meetings, and learned about government pensions for retired people. Progressives had not yet achieved these rights and benefits in the United States.

She wrote to a friend, "I had very little money, and when I found what a delightful, restful country it is, I wanted to stay, so I went out sewing by the day. It was such a splendid way to learn of the living conditions of the people." She didn't have a full-time job, but she worked for a seamstress shop and earned daily wages for the days she worked. Because people were curious about Americans, they gave Jeannette their business. She charged twice the normal rate and urged other seamstresses to do the same. Inspired by Jeannette, her co-workers raised their prices and doubled their pay!

After nearly a year, Jeannette returned to Montana in 1916. What should she do next? She could take up suffrage work again, since only twelve of the forty-eight states allowed women to vote. Or perhaps she could work for peace. World War I had started in Europe, and Jeannette protested in a most unladylike way: "If they are going to have war, they ought to take the old men and leave the young to propagate the race." In those days, "polite" women didn't discuss "propagating the race," even as a joke. But another idea came to her, something that would let her work for all the issues she cared about.

She could run for Congress.

She asked her suffragist friends in Montana about her plan. They didn't like it. She would certainly lose the election and disgrace their work. Perhaps she could run for a less important office, like the state legislature. Jeannette had upset eastern suffrage leaders like Carrie Chapman Catt by sometimes disagreeing with their policies. But Jeannette had made up her mind. "I told the eastern women that maybe I wasn't the best person to be the first [female] congressman, but I could be elected." She wasn't a lawyer or an

Jeannette stands with her brother, Wellington, outside their home in Missoula. He declared that he would manage her campaign for Congress and she would win. He was right.

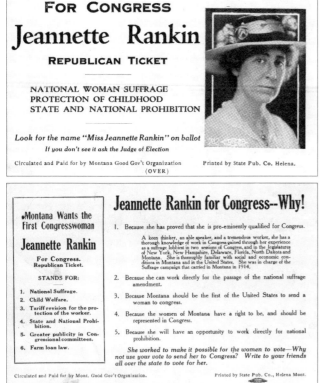

Jeannette and her staff scattered these campaign cards all across Montana to convince voters—both men and women—to vote for her.

intellectual, but she was a first-class campaigner. She knew how to talk to people and how to organize her followers.

This would be the biggest adventure of her life. For years she had been saying that women were smart enough, strong enough, brave enough to enter politics. Then, in 1916 at age thirty-six, she had to prove it.

Her family stood behind her. Wellington, Harriet, and Mary were in their thirties; Grace and Edna, in their twenties. They had all graduated from college and built independent lives of their own. Wellington was on his way to becoming one of the most powerful and wealthy lawyers in Montana. Mary taught English at the university in Missoula. Harriet would become the dean of women there. Edna became the first woman lawyer born in Montana, and Grace raised a family of three children. Jeannette's siblings rallied round her. Her four sisters left families, jobs, and university studies for a few months to campaign for Jeannette. As for Wellington, he said, "I'll manage your campaign and you'll be elected."

The Rankin men had always registered as Republicans, but Jeannette belonged to no political party. Formed in the mid-nineteenth century, the Republican Party had been the liberal party of Lincoln, opposed to slavery. By the twentieth century it had become the conservative party of big business, though Republican President Theodore Roosevelt had supported laws to break up large corporations that forced small companies out of business. Generally speaking, Northern middle-class, native-born Protestants tended to support the Republican Party. Southerners, immigrants, Catholics, and the working classes often supported the Democrats. As for Jeannette, "I never was a Republican. ... I ran on the Republican ticket." She would vote for what she believed in, regardless of party politics.

First she ran against seven other Republican candidates in a primary election. The top two vote getters would run in the November election. Jeannette received 22,549 votes. Her nearest rival got 15,469. She was on her way.

Most Montana newspapers were controlled by the Anaconda Copper Mining Company, which opposed everything Jeannette supported—labor unions, better working conditions, and rights for women. None of these newspapers printed any news of her campaign. It didn't matter. Montanans had heard about Jeannette Rankin through her suffrage work, and they flocked to hear her speak. She traveled all around her large state by car and by train, even once or twice in a horse and buggy.

She spoke about issues that politicians didn't often talk about. "There are hundreds of men [in Congress] to care for the nation's tariff and foreign policy and irrigation projects. But there isn't a single woman to look after the nation's greatest asset: its children."

Jeannette Rankin campaigned as a woman for women. War and peace were not her main issues in this election. World War I was raging in Europe, and she didn't want the United States entering the war.

> ## BRASS BANDS GREET
> ## JEANETTE RANKIN ALL OVER STATE
> ### Political Trappings of the Good Old Days
> ### Are Revived for Woman Candidate
>
> Brass bands and street parades and all the good old-fashioned fancy trimmings that used to go with significant political meetings are being revived in honor of Jeanette Rankin, Montana's first woman to run for a seat in the United States congress. Open-air meetings are being held in every county and Jeanette Rankin clubs are being organized all over the state.
>
> *Kalispell Times*
> Kalispell, Montana
> August 17, 1916

Jeannette received a warm welcome all over the state—even if the newspapers didn't always spell her name right!

from **WHAT I EXPECT TO DO WHEN I GET TO CONGRESS**

Several years ago during a session of Congress, $300,000 was appropriated for the study of fodder for hogs. At the same session $30,000 was appropriated for a study of the needs of the nation's children.

It would seem that in the eyes of Congress the hogs of the nation are ten times more important than [children]. … [U]ntil now we haven't had a woman in our National Legislature to do for the nation's most precious asset, its children, what the men have been doing for the hogs.

Jeannette Rankin
New York Sunday American
November 26, 1916

President Woodrow Wilson, running for election to a second term, used the campaign slogan "He kept us out of war." Jeannette and many others believed he would continue that policy. So she focused on women's suffrage and children's welfare. She seemed unaware that in May 1916 Wilson asked Congress for money to build more battleships and double the size of the army. Congress gave him what he wanted.

Montana didn't have different congressional districts with one congressman in each. The whole state had two representatives-at-large. That meant that all Montana voters voted for two candidates. Jeannette ran against one other Republican, two Democrats, and two Socialists. She didn't run a dirty campaign, insulting the men who ran against her. Wherever she went, she urged voters to vote for their local man and for her.

On November 6, 1916, Jeannette voted for the first time—for herself. That night she called the newspaper office to find out the election results. Without giving her name she asked if President Woodrow Wilson had won in Montana. Yes, Wilson had won. What about Jeannette Rankin? No, she had lost. Jeannette was crushed.

The next morning the paper reported her defeat, but Wellington wasn't convinced. All the votes hadn't been counted yet, and he predicted his sister would win. He was right. Voters in the cities had favored her opponents. Perhaps they were influenced by business interests and the newspapers that Anaconda Mining owned. For three days Jeannette waited anxiously for the final tally of votes. Finally she learned that women, farmers, and miners in the rural districts made Jeannette Rankin the first woman elected to the United States House of Representatives. In fact, she was the first woman elected to any democratic lawmaking body in the world! "I knew the women would stand by me," said Jeannette.

Newspaper reporters and photographers from across the United States and as far away as Europe rushed to Missoula and stood outside the Rankin family house. Voters in Montana had seen and heard Jeannette, but she was unknown to the outside world. Now everyone wanted interviews and photographs of the most famous woman of the day. Stacks of letters and telegrams arrived from all over the world. Marriage proposals came from strangers who believed she needed a husband. An automobile company promised her a free car, and a toothpaste company offered her five thousand dollars to smile in its ads. She turned everyone down and wouldn't even come out of her house until the photographers and reporters went away.

They had to imagine what she was like. Some stories described a glamour girl, others a young innocent "slip" of a thing. Some expected a rough, aggressive woman, and others a pistol-packing cowgirl. Wellington reported, "Her life is devoted to the cause of mankind and government, first, last and always." But Jeannette was more colorful than that.

A Montana rancher declared, "Jeannette will make 'em sit up and take notice. She comes from fighting stock and carries a kick in her arguments." Not only that, she had earned two college degrees, traveled the entire country

The Congresslady

We have so many Congressmen
Whose ways are dark and shady—
How joyfully we welcome then
The coming Congresslady!

I wonder, is she old and stout
Or is she young and pretty?
How long the members will stay out
Who are on her committee!

We'll hear no more of shabbiness
Among our legislators—
She'll make them formal in their dress
They'll wear boiled shirts and gaiters.

Her maiden speeches will be known
For charm and grace of manner;
But who on earth will chaperone
The member from Montana?

Christopher Morley
New York Times Sunday Magazine
November 19, 1916

Jeannette gave a speech from National American Woman Suffrage Association (NAWSA) headquarters in Washington, D.C., on April 2, 1917, her first day in Congress. Behind her stands Carrie Chapman Catt, president of NAWSA, who often quarreled with Jeannette.

several times, lived abroad, and knew how to talk to lawmakers as well as people on the street. At thirty-six years old, she was ready for her great adventure.

When she did speak to reporters, she showed them what a confident politician she already was.

I'm not nervous about going to Congress. Why should I be? Because I shall be the only woman there as a member, is no reason why I should hesitate or falter in the performance of my duty there, any more than anywhere else.

Of course I shall make speeches. I've been making them for the last eight years, for suffrage, for prohibition and for myself. But I am more concerned in social welfare legislation. My work and study in the Children's Home Society [in Washington State] gave me a good insight into the needs of babies, children and young adults, and it is for them that I shall work especially. My experience in politics ought to help me to do this with a goodly measure of success.

Though Jeannette showed a confident face to the world, she was worried. On her first day in Congress, America's leading suffragists held a formal breakfast for her. Ten speakers praised her past work and placed their hopes in her for the future. Some women in the audience wore white armbands, showing they opposed U.S. involvement in World War I. Jeannette, too, opposed the war, yet her primary concern was women's suffrage. In a speech a month earlier she had sidestepped the war issue and said, "Women ought to have a right to say whether their men shall go to war." In other words, let women vote for the congressmen who decide.

The war had bitterly divided the suffragists. Some pacifists had spoken out against it, while others believed it was worth fighting. Still others refused to take a stand on the war, believing the issue would damage the cause of suffrage. How could Jeannette satisfy all groups?

When she finally stood to speak to the women who honored her on this historic occasion, she said, "There will be many times when I will make mistakes. And I need your encouragement and your support. I know I will get it. I promise—I promise—" She couldn't continue and sat down. For once, she was lost for words. What could she promise?

Besides, the time for words and promises was past. Now, on her first day in Congress, she had to act. President Wilson was going to ask for a declaration of war.

WORLD WAR I

The issues that led to World War I (1914–1918) were varied and complex. During the 1800s, nationalism became an important force in Europe. Both Italy and Germany formed nations from many small independent states. Nationalist groups ruled by the old Austro-Hungarian Empire and the Russian Empire wanted to break away and form nations of their own. Germany, France, and Great Britain had taken over large parts of Africa and Asia to create overseas empires and competed for the economic riches of these lands. World trade became more important, and economic and political conflicts grew among nations.

In August 1914 war broke out—the biggest, bloodiest war the world had ever known. Great Britain, France, and later the United States led the Allies. They fought against Germany, Austria-Hungary, and the Ottoman Empire—the Central powers.

Four years later, with ten million people dead and twenty million wounded, the Central powers surrendered. Epidemics and starvation killed millions more. New weapons technology—poison gas, submarines, tanks, and airplanes—helped to make the war more deadly than previous wars. People vowed that it would be "the war to end all wars." And yet, twenty years later, the world was at war once again.

CHAPTER SIX

"I Cannot Vote for War."

WHEN JEANNETTE RANKIN WALKED into the House of Representatives for the first time on April 2, 1917, everyone rose. In the visitor's gallery her mother and brother smiled proudly. Jeannette carried a bouquet of yellow and purple flowers, the colors of the Congressional Union, the pacifist group of suffragists. As she made her way through the hall to her seat, congressmen rushed to shake her hand. She graciously smiled at them all. When the clerk called the roll and came to "Rankin, Montana," she stood up and bowed first to the Republicans and then to the Democrats while everyone applauded.

Ellen Maury Slayden, a congressman's wife, watched the scene and wrote in her diary:

> Not more than a year ago men would say ... "Next thing you'll be wanting women in Congress," as if that was the reductio ad absurdum, and here she was coming in, escorted by an elderly colleague [Rep. John Evans of Montana], looking like a mature bride

On her first day in Congress, April 2, 1917, Jeannette Rankin holds a bouquet of purple and yellow flowers, colors of the Congressional Union, a suffragist group that opposed the war.

rather than a strong-minded female, and the men were clapping and cheering in the friendliest way. ... She was a sensible young woman going about her business.

And serious business lay ahead. A few minutes later President Wilson asked Congress to declare war on Germany and fight on the side of Great Britain and France. "The world must be made safe for democracy," he said.

Jeannette Rankin, the first female member of Congress, sat in this audience and heard President Woodrow Wilson ask for a declaration of war against Germany.

When war first began in Europe in 1914, Wilson had offered to negotiate a peace treaty between the warring nations. He said that "the United States must be neutral in fact as well as in name during these days that are to try men's souls." He wanted Americans to be "impartial in thought as well as in action." But as the war progressed, American sympathies leaned toward the Allies—Great Britain and France—and against the Central powers—Germany and Austria. U.S. banks gave huge loans to the Allies. U.S. businesses made enormous profits selling military equipment and other supplies to the Allies. To stop this trade, at the end of 1916 Germany declared that its submarines would attack any ship bound for England or France, including American ones. President Wilson cut official ties with Germany, and then, on April 2, 1917, he asked the United States to go to war in Europe.

For the next three days, Congress hotly debated the issue far into the night. Most spoke in favor of war, patriotism, and manly courage. Claude Kitchin, Democratic leader of the House, objected, saying, "... [L]et me at once remind the House that it takes neither moral nor physical courage to declare a war for others to fight."

Jeannette was bombarded with advice from every side. Pacifist suffragists like Alice Paul wanted her to vote against the war. Others, like Carrie Chapman Catt, wanted her to put women's suffrage first and

In her office, Jeannette studied bills she would vote on in Congress, answered mail from her constituents in Montana, and met with visitors who dropped in to visit that new species: congresswoman.

Jeannette received more mail than any other member of Congress. Her staff typed form letters like this one to answer most of her mail.

support the president and the war. Some suffrage supporters and their opponents said a vote against war would prove that she—and all women—wasn't brave enough to sit in Congress. Her brother, Wellington, warned that she would never get reelected if she voted against the war.

Now she listened to her fellow congressmen. She herself opposed war. But she had not made up her mind about this vote. She would wait until the final moments to vote, and "if I could see any reason for going to war I would try to change." Finally, after three days of debate, at two o'clock in the morning, the vote was taken. State by state, the clerk read the names of the members of Congress. Each representative answered aloud aye or no. When the clerk called "Rankin," she stood and said, "I want to stand by my country, but I cannot vote for war."

Though fifty-five other congressmen also voted against entering World War I, Jeannette Rankin received the strongest criticism. The National American Woman Suffrage Association, a group that Jeannette had worked for, canceled a reception planned for her. Carrie Chapman Catt, head of the group, said publicly, "Miss Rankin was not voting for the suffragists of the nation; she represents Montana." Privately, she wrote, "Our Congress Lady is a sure enough joker. … Every time she answers a roll call she looses [sic] us a million votes." Wellington said, "She would consider it more dishonest not to vote your conviction than it would be to rob a bank." Years later, Jeannette said, "I knew it would be a popular war. I knew I would not be re-elected. … I voted my conscience."

Two sacks of mail—about three hundred letters—arrived for Jeannette each day. Not all letters were critical. Many people thanked her for her courageous vote. But others declared she was not fit to serve in Congress and should resign. Jeannette had no intention of quitting. She had work to do. "We did not labor in suffrage just to bring the vote to women, but to allow women to express their opinions and become effective in government."

She never regretted her first vote in Congress. Rather, she saw it as perhaps the best vote she ever cast. Many years later she said,

I believe that the first vote I cast was the most significant vote and a most significant act on the part of women, because women are going to have to stop war. I felt at the time that the first woman [in Congress] should take the first stand, that the first time the first woman had a chance to say no to war she should say it. That was what held me up with all the pressures being brought to get me to vote for war.

Jeannette had rented a large apartment in Washington, D.C., and filled it with co-workers and family. Her mother, Olive, lived with her. Two

IDEAS THAT THE CONGRESSWOMAN BRINGS

This political cartoon shows some "baggage" Jeannette took to Congress.

Congressional work sometimes took Jeannette out of her office. Here she plants a Montana fir tree on the Capitol grounds on Arbor Day, 1917.

Jeannette was the only congressional representative with an all-female staff.

The Anaconda Copper Mining Company was the most powerful economic and political force in Montana. The company opposed Jeannette and everything she supported: trade unions, better wages and working conditions for workers, and a limit to wartime profits.

of her female assistants, who answered the thousands of letters sent to Jeannette, lived there until Jeannette's sister Harriet and her two young children moved in. Harriet's husband had died suddenly and Jeannette offered her sister a home and a job. She became Jeannette's office manager. Jeannette also had two more employees, which gave her a larger office staff than any other representative. But then she got more mail than anyone else. She was the only congressperson with an all-female staff.

Belle Winestine, a friend from Montana, became Jeannette's ghostwriter. Jeannette didn't like to write and found it tedious, so Belle took Jeannette's sketchy notes and wrote magazine and newspaper articles for her. Though Jeannette was a powerful public speaker, she never wrote out her speeches. Sometimes others wrote them for her, but even then, she would often stray from the written words and make up a speech as she went along.

Perhaps Jeannette's boldest action was speaking out against the mighty Anaconda Copper Mining Company. Anaconda mined 20 percent of the nation's copper in its Butte, Montana, mines. Copper was essential for the weapons used in World War I, and the mining companies were making huge profits. A fire in a Butte mine in June 1917 killed 168 men. Their bodies were found by blocked-up exits that would have allowed the men to escape. The companies in Montana had been warned of safety violations but had really done nothing. The miners went on strike, which was illegal, for better working conditions. They tried to form a labor union, but the mining companies, led by Anaconda, refused to allow it.

The miners appealed to Jeannette, asking her to speak to the national Department of Labor. She did that and also spoke to President Wilson. They refused to help. So Jeannette went to Montana herself to set up talks between Anaconda and the miners. She told reporters,

I think I know perfectly well what [Anaconda] will try to do to me. It'll try to do to me just what it has done to every one who ever tried to oppose it in and out of Montana. It owns the state. It owns the government. It owns the press.

First, I'll be roasted from one end of the state to the other. Every newspaper will print my shortcomings, real or fancied, in the largest type in the composing room. All the mud and all the bricks in the state will come hurling in my direction.

The company did all that and more. When she traveled back to Montana to meet with striking workers and company officials, the company hired policemen to prevent her from speaking to the crowd that was waiting for her. So she met union leaders and local government officials in private. The mining company refused to talk to her at all. Jeannette wanted the federal government to take over the running of the mines until the war ended, but all her efforts failed. Eventually the miners went back to work, without a union. It was a bitter defeat for Jeannette.

She had more success with working women. The Bureau of Printing and Engraving in Washington, D.C., hired many women to print Liberty Loan Bonds. These bonds, bought by ordinary Americans, were a kind of savings account. The government paid interest on the bonds and used the funds to finance the war. Federal law said that women printers could work

Many women worked in the Bureau of Printing and Engraving in Washington, D.C., printing money and Liberty Bonds. During World War I, they turned to Jeannette when working conditions grew worse.

only eight hours a day. But the bureau forced them to work as much as fifteen hours a day and canceled their vacation time.

A group of workers came to Jeannette for help. First she toured the printing plant, disguised as a tourist. Then she hired a private detective to investigate working conditions. Finally, she spoke to the bureau director and told him to restore the eight-hour workday, or she would call for an investigation by Congress. The director held his own investigation and restored vacations and an eight-hour day. The workers, encouraged by Jeannette, went on to organize a labor union.

Plate-Printer, the national journal of printing employees, declared, "The great army of labor did not realize that in sending Miss Rankin to Washington, Montana was sending an angel in disguise, the woman we love best in all the world."

When the House of Representatives debated the issue of a constitutional amendment for women's right to vote, Jeannette was the first to speak. As always, she was bold and articulate.

It is time for our old political doctrines to give way to the new visions. ... Deep down in the hearts of the American people is a living faith in democracy. ... It is our national religion, and it prompts in us the desire for that measure of justice which is based on equal opportunity, equal protection, equal freedom for all.

She closed her speech by asking, "[H]ow shall we explain ... the meaning of democracy if the same Congress that voted for war to make the world safe for democracy refuses to give this small measure of democracy to the women of our country?" The House passed the suffrage measure by just one vote and Jeannette was overjoyed—for a moment. Then the Senate defeated the bill.

Upholding the democratic rights she held dear, Jeannette voted against laws that took away freedom of speech during wartime. But these laws passed anyway and legalized censorship of the press and public speaking. German Americans were suspected of being traitors. Antiwar protesters were labeled unpatriotic and some landed in jail.

She cosponsored a health bill for women and children, and another bill against child labor. Not one of Rankin's progressive bills—women's suffrage, workers' rights, health and social welfare, equal pay for women—passed while she was in Congress, but many of them did eventually become law. "I have always regretted that there was no opportunity for really constructive legislation. There never is in wartime. So many things I was interested in, it was impossible to work on." Jeannette, the pioneer from Montana, was also a pioneer in Congress. But she had to wait for the times to catch up with her.

Once war had been declared, Jeannette voted for many of the military bills in Congress because she wanted America to win—and end—the war as quickly as possible. But Montanans remembered her "no" vote. When she returned home to sell Liberty Loan Bonds to finance the war, she literally found doors locked against her. In one town she had to speak in a park during a snowstorm, clinging to

World War I soldiers spent months, even years, living and fighting in trenches like this.

The U.S. government issued Liberty Bonds to raise money to pay for World War I. Though Jeannette Rankin opposed the war, she wanted the country to win as quickly as possible, so she encouraged people to buy Liberty Bonds.

a fence to avoid being blown over.

Wartime brought hardship to Americans. All men between eighteen and thirty-five had to register for the draft. The army had 200,000 men when war was declared. When it ended in late 1918, the armed forces numbered nearly 5,000,000. More than half of these men had been drafted into service. Jeannette tried to reduce the hardships for the soldiers and the families they left behind. She introduced bills in Congress to help Montana farmers get federal loans and reduce their costs. She telegraphed a Montana newspaper editor, saying, "Am bending every effort toward relief of Montana farmers, appreciating that assistance is necessary if Montana is to make that contribution to the nation's food supply which is necessary to the successful conduct of the war." She wanted to relax rules for homesteaders who had joined the army. She tried to get payments for families of soldiers. On Sunday evenings she cooked dinner for young Montana soldiers on their way to Europe. For some, it was the last home cooking they ate before they died in muddy trenches in France.

Jeannette's term in Congress ended in 1918, and she didn't try to get reelected to the House of Representatives. Montana had formed new congressional districts, and Missoula, her Montana home, was in a solidly Democratic area. She ran for the U.S. Senate instead, since voters all over Montana voted for senators. But nearly everyone had turned against her—the Republican Party, leading women suffragists, even the voters. She ran again as a Republican but lost the primary election in a close race. She continued her campaign for the Senate as a National Party candidate, a party formed of several reform groups. In the general election she came in last.

Congress had been the ideal place for Jeannette. It gave her a chance to use her broad intelligence and good people skills to work for change in society. Yet that door now slammed shut. What would she do next?

Women thought deeply about the harm that war brought to American life. In February 1915, The Ladies' Home Journal *published an essay that spoke of the lessons Americans could learn from the war.*
1. *Americans must change their spending habits. They waste too much money on extravagant luxuries.*
2. *The United States is part of a global family of nations, not a world-dominating force that is independent of other countries.*
3. *Parents should not allow children to play war games with guns.*
4. *Women can create peace and end war in the larger world by teaching the values of peace at home and in the classroom.*

Before World War I, people were thinking of the future and of changing things that were wrong. The women were asking for the vote and the men were asking for workman's compensation. ... All the people were thinking of a world at peace, and the things that could be done to give the people a greater expression in their government. ... And war came and destroyed everything. It divided people. It divided the women—those who wanted the war and those who didn't want it.

Jeannette Rankin

CHAPTER SEVEN

Fighting for Peace

Jeannette traveled to Europe for a meeting of the Women's International League for Peace and Freedom. Here she sits in the front row wearing a wide dark hat. Jane Addams, her friend and mentor, sits two persons to her left.

JEANNETTE LOST HER JOB IN CONGRESS, BUT SHE LOST NONE OF HER passion for politics. In 1919 she traveled to Europe with a group of twenty-six American women, including her hero, Jane Addams. Women from sixteen countries met in Zürich, Switzerland, for the Second International Congress of Women for Permanent Peace. Jane Addams took a special liking to Jeannette. Jeannette was thirty-eight, Addams, twenty years older. Addams was a teacher, a role model, and a sort of elder sister for Jeannette.

"Miss Addams was wonderful to me," Jeannette said. "She used to have me sit next to her at her table. … When she had callers she always had someone with her, and she always took me. … Those were wonderful times!" Of all the remarkable women Jeannette knew, she admired Jane Addams most. "She was a perfect blend of thought and action. She had a grasp of economics, finance, law, administration, international affairs, everything. She should have been president," declared Jeannette.

Soldiers on horseback and crowds of mourners visit the American Cemetery in Suresnes, France, on Memorial Day, May 30, 1920. Jeannette Rankin visited cemeteries like this in France in 1919. They served to strengthen her commitment to building a permanent peace.

Before the women's congress began in May 1919, Jeannette visited the desolate battlefields of France with Addams and a few others. France had "won" the war. Yet the women saw ruined farm fields still littered with rusting barbed wire, and vast cemeteries filled with dead soldiers. They also saw starving children on the streets of Paris. Jeannette was so shocked by these sights of the "winners" that she didn't go to Germany with Addams to visit the "losers." As far as Jeannette could see, everyone had lost.

The women had no political power, but they wanted to discuss ways to prevent war in the future. World War I had ended in November 1918 with Germany's surrender. Officials—all men—from the winning countries met in France to decide how to punish the losers. The women also wanted to meet in France, but the French government refused them permission because they had invited delegates from the defeated nations. When these German and Austrian women arrived at the congress in May 1919, Jane Addams was appalled. She had met these vigorous, beautiful women several years before and was now shocked by their emaciated state.

France had won World War I but was left with ruined towns and cities. Jeannette saw sights like this cathedral in Soissons, France, which had been bombed during the war.

Germans and other Eastern Europeans were starving. Famine and disease had hit their countries hard, in part because the Allies had set up a blockade against food shipments. The women's congress sent a telegram to the men meeting in France, demanding that food, money, and supplies be sent immediately to all people in need. President Wilson was the only leader who responded. "Your message appeals to my head and my heart," he replied. But he did nothing.

In discussions about the defeated nations, Jeannette said, "… [O]pen the channels of communication and let them do as they please." Unlike the men, the women talked not about punishment, but about how to promote peace and prosperity to prevent future wars.

The men ignored the women and forced Germany to make large financial payments, give up German territory, accept occupying armies in Germany for fifteen years, and severely limit its military forces. The women's peace congress rejected these harsh terms of peace. The women had no power to enforce their principles, but they supported a resolution introduced by Jeannette Rankin and Ethel Snowden of England. Their statement read:

> *This International Congress of Women expresses its deep regret that the terms of peace proposed at Versailles should so seriously violate the principles upon which alone a just and lasting peace can be secured, and which the democracies of the world had come to accept. [T]he terms of peace … create all over Europe discords and animosities which can only lead to future wars. … By the financial and economic proposals a hundred million people of this generation in the heart of Europe are condemned to poverty, dis-*

ease and despair, which must result in the spread of hatred and anarchy within each nation.

History proved the women right. The conditions that the men demanded created economic hardship and deep resentment among the Germans. This helped to bring about the rise of Adolph Hitler and the Nazi Party dictatorship.

With the war over, suffragists increased their activity, and in June 1919 Congress passed the Nineteenth Amendment to the Constitution. It stated that "The right of citizens of the United States to vote shall not be denied or abridged by the United States or by any State on account of sex." A year later, in August 1920, the required three-fourths of the states in the union had ratified it. All women in the United States could vote.

Jeannette Rankin, with handbag in the front row, had proposed a bill in Congress to provide health care for mothers and children. The bill did not pass at that time. However, she worked with other women, shown here, to persuade Congress to pass similar legislation in 1921.

Jeannette thought that peace would reign now. "It was women's work which was destroyed by war. Their work was raising human beings, and war destroyed humans to protect profits and property." Jeannette and others believed that women would never vote for politicians who wanted war. How wrong they were!

Jeannette, now forty, began to work full-time for social reform. If she couldn't get elected to Congress, she would try to influence politicians as a private citizen. She worked for the Women's International League for Peace and Freedom (WILPF), the group that had met in Zürich. She lobbied in Washington to secure the swift release of prisoners of war and political prisoners, those arrested for speaking out against government policy during the war. Some of these political prisoners were pacifists. But pacifists were not in charge of the government, and Jeannette's work did not succeed.

She next worked for the National Consumers' League (NCL), lobbying for the Maternity and Infancy Care Act, also known as the Sheppard-Towner Act, in Congress—much like the one she had introduced—providing health care for mothers and children. This time the bill passed. For four years she toured the country working for more laws to protect families and workers. She gave speeches and organized local groups, as she had done for women's suffrage. She lobbied congressmen in Washington.

But the Progressive era was over. President Calvin Coolidge claimed that "the chief business of the American people is business," and lawmakers agreed with him in the 1920s. Social reform might cut into profits. In 1924 Jeannette resigned her position at NCL to work for peace.

Jeannette stands in front of her small house in Georgia, quite different from the elegant Rankin home in Missoula, Montana.

She needed a home base. Montana was too far from Washington, so she bought a sixty-four-acre farm near Athens, Georgia, with a small cabin and a screened porch. It had no electricity or running water, just an outhouse. Her niece Dorothy remembered the outhouse well. "I felt very sorry for myself, since we had *The Nation* and *The New Republic* [progressive political journals] for toilet paper, and very rough paper it was, while all our neighbors wiped on catalogues with slick paper."

Many friends came to visit Jeannette's farm, including women from the old Heterodoxy Club in New York City. One wrote several articles about such a visit and published them in *Woman's Home Companion* in 1926. "[Jeannette] always had guests, and no matter how many nor how brief their stay she spread her wings and hovered [over] them like one large family."

The farm was a paradise of honey-suckle vines and dogwood trees. Tall pines surrounded the little house. Her friend wrote, "[Jeannette] cherished her trees as some women cherish diamonds. She cleared away only the dead ones, and woe to anybody who snapped a green branch or broke a living shoot. I think she knew by name every tree on her land."

Mockingbirds and turtledoves sang in the trees. Wild cherry and wild plum trees dropped their fruit in late spring. Dew-berries and figs ripened in the summer. Grapes and persimmons sweetened the fall. All summer Jeannette kept the ket-tles boiling to can fruit and make jam. Jeannette took her farming seriously. She planted velvet beans to enrich the soil. She consulted a state agricultural

Jeannette's close friend, author Katharine Anthony, visited her in Georgia and in 1926 published a series of illustrated articles about Jeannette's life there. This drawing shows Jeannette buying grapes from the neighborhood boys.

agent about her pecans and peaches, the glory of the farm. Two hundred pecan trees and eight hundred peach trees brought her some income and the satisfaction of working the land, just as her parents and grandpar-ents had done. Jeannette still had her small monthly income from her inheritance, a small salary from her work as a peace activist, and occa-sional gifts from her brother. She didn't need much money to live the life she had chosen in Georgia.

During her term in Congress, Jeannette became close friends with fellow congressman Fiorello LaGuardia, who later became New York City's most popular mayor. During the 1920s, their friendship deepened and LaGuardia told one of Jeannette's sisters, "You don't know how hard I tried to get this gal [Jeannette] to marry me." She always turned him down, but they remained close friends all their lives.

Fiorello LaGuardia met Jeannette in Congress in 1916, and they remained close friends. He claimed he proposed to Jeannette many times, but she always turned him down. Was he serious or only joking? Jeannette never said.

Olive Rankin sits surrounded by her large family in 1920. Her children stand in the back row, left to right: Harriet, Mary, Wellington, Edna, Grace, and Jeannette. Neither Jeannette nor Wellington had children, but their four sisters gave them many nieces and nephews.

Jeannette never married, but she kept close to her family. Her mother moved to Georgia to help Jeannette raise her sister Edna's children, Dorothy and John, after Edna divorced. Olive Rankin cared for the children when Jeannette's work took her away from home. Some years they escaped the hot Georgia summers and drove to Montana. Jeannette grieved deeply when her nephew John died in a summer camp accident at age seven. As for Dorothy, Jeannette treated her like a daughter all her life.

Jeannette made friends with neighborhood children, too. She formed the Sunshine Club for girls, and the members paid dues and elected officers. Perhaps Jeannette was training them for professional careers. But they had fun, too, baking bread and swimming in a nearby pond. The boys' club was less organized—no officers, dues, or even regular members. Jeannette told them stories about places she had visited, and the boys played noisy games of tag. In the fall, the boys picked grapes and sold them by the bucketful. Jeannette knew they used the money to buy schoolbooks, and she became their biggest customer.

Jeannette spent her time in Georgia fixing up her house, tending her farm, and being neighborly. Her only vacations seemed to be summers in Montana, where she stayed on Wellington's ranch, taking charge of a large household of her mother, siblings, and their children. Jeannette still loved the country where she grew up. "From our front window we can see thirty miles to the sunset, and on the north it is hard to see the top of the mountain from the window. On the south we slope down to Lake Sewell which is part of the Missouri River, where we have a darling cabin and lovely beach to swim."

She fished in the river and took long horseback rides after dinner. She retreated to a little shack and spent long hours reading and thinking. When fall arrived, as she had done in Georgia, Jeannette organized a canning brigade. "We have over 200 quarts of applesauce alone, besides several hundred glasses of jelly and apple butter and pickles … [and] a hundred pounds of luscious, big tomatoes begging to be picked," she wrote to her friends. Jeannette's career as a social justice activist often took her to big cities, and she thrived in those centers of power. But another part of her came alive in the country—Georgia and Montana—where she lived close to the earth.

In Georgia, she organized not only the children in her neighborhood but the adults as well. She founded the Georgia Peace Society to find ways to prepare for peace, like nations prepared for war.

The peace groups of the 1920s and 1930s

In 1926 Katharine Anthony described how Jeannette's "girls' club" enjoyed swimming on a hot Georgia afternoon.

During the 1920s and 1930s, Jeannette gave talks to "prepare for peace" as she saw nations preparing for war. Though Jeannette "dressed down" on her farm in Georgia, she dressed up when she spoke in public—and still wore a hat.

attracted a tiny minority of the total population, but their commitment to peace kept them going. They tried to obtain a constitutional amendment making warfare illegal but failed. They supported international actions to reduce the size of nations' military forces and failed. They worked with Senator Gerald Nye on his Senate Munitions Investigating Committee into the U.S. actions in World War I. As Jeannette had suspected, corruption and greed had played a part. Weapons makers and bankers had influenced the government's decision to enter the war.

During this time, Jeannette worked for several peace groups. When she wasn't working with Senator Nye and others in Washington, she traveled around the country. She made speeches on the new medium, the radio. But she had disagreements with some peace groups. She knew from the women's suffrage movement that you couldn't breeze into a town, make speeches, and leave. "I … said you had to organize and you had to go back and see that the organization worked. … [Y]ou had to take a certain amount of territory and *make it solid*."

During the 1930s, Jeannette Rankin worked with Senator Gerald Nye from North Dakota to promote the cause of peace. They helped to persuade Congress to pass the Neutrality Acts that prevented the United States from taking sides for a few years in the growing European conflict.

Though Jeannette Rankin worked for peace, she wasn't a total pacifist. She believed in an army to defend the country against invasion, but not to fight in foreign lands. Jeannette had never joined a church. Her commitment to peace came not from religious faith, but from a moral belief in solving problems without violence. A minister once pressed her to explain why she was a pacifist. Finally she replied, "Just stubborn, I guess."

There was more to it, though. Her father's nonviolent attitudes toward American Indians had influenced her. The Progressive reformers' goal to build a better society appealed to her. Perhaps most of all, Jeannette's years of speaking on street corners and in halls of government, using words rather than weapons, working with people rather than against them, convinced her that peaceful negotiation was the way to resolve conflicts and promote the well-being of all people.

Jeannette's stubbornness certainly helped her, as she repeated her peace

THE WHITE HOUSE
WASHINGTON

November 13, 1933

My dear Miss Rankin:

At present it is very difficult
to deal with Germany normally or ration-
ally, because while she is demanding that
other nations disarm, she herself is
arming in every way she can under cover.
I think the only thing we can do at this
time is to keep people as calm as possible -
the women especially - in all countries.
If the will for peace can grow in the
hearts of women everywhere we may be able
to bridge over the present tense situation
in Europe.

Very sincerely yours,

Eleanor Roosevelt

Jeannette took her pursuit of peace as far as the White House. In this letter, First Lady Eleanor Roosevelt echoes Jeannette's own belief that women can provide a strong voice for peace.

Police in New York City hand out eggs and bread to people in 1930 at the start of the Great Depression. General prosperity did not return to the United States until after World War II.

The Great Depression of the 1930s brought vast unemployment. President Roosevelt's New Deal created jobs for some people. Here a group of demonstrators in 1935 demand work.

message again … and again … and again. In 1932 she took her peace show on the road. She organized a peace march from Washington, D.C., to Chicago, where Democrats and Republicans held conventions to choose candidates for presidential elections that year. The caravan of cars traveled over eight hundred miles, stopping in towns and cities to speak out for peace. Many college students joined in, along with disabled veterans from World War I.

The Chicago peace parades went smoothly, but the two political parties cared more about finding ways to ease the Great Depression.

These Brenau College (Georgia) students invited Jeannette Rankin to speak to them about promoting peace. The American Legion, a conservative group of veterans, accused Jeannette of preaching "un-American doctrines to the young womanhood of the South. ..." The young women stoutly defended Jeannette's ideas and their right to listen to her.

An economic crash in 1929 had ended a time of prosperity in the United States. Many businesses and banks failed, and millions of people lost their jobs. The issue of war and peace didn't seem important to most people in 1932.

Two years later, Jeannette, now fifty-four, gave a series of peace lectures at Brenau College, a women's college in Georgia. The college wanted to establish a Chair of Peace, with Jeannette as the first professor. In Atlanta an American Legion post—a group of conservative army veterans—attacked the plan, claiming it was "detrimental to the welfare of American youth." In addition, they claimed that "pacifists [were] closely akin to communists and that no good could come ... [from allowing Jeannette] to preach un-American doctrines to the young womanhood of the South ..."

Many southern newspapers took Jeannette's side. The Brenau College paper proclaimed, "We say welcome to Miss Rankin. Welcome to all those whose desire it is to build of America a more wonderful nation."

Jeannette spoke out. "The sum of my reputed radicalism seems to be my opposition to war, to competitive armaments, and to predatory inter-

It is not patriotism which prompts war, but greed and gain. Wars are started by those who want to make profit, yet we send our sons to die for that.

Jeannette Rankin
The Atlanta Georgian
October 13, 1934

ests. I have no quarrel with the American Legion. I grant them the same American and constitutional freedom of conscience and freedom of speech which I claim for myself."

The Brenau plan for a Chair of Peace died for lack of money. But the attacks against Jeannette continued for a year, until the *Macon Evening News* called Jeannette a communist. She had had enough. She sued the journalist and the newspaper for libel, publishing false information. It took another year of legal battles, but finally the Macon newspaper printed an apology to Jeannette on the front page.

Jeannette worked for ten years (1929–1939) for the National Council for the Prevention of War under Frederick Libby. He had started the organization and raised most of its money from a variety of church groups and wealthy people. Jeannette, with her knowledge of the ways of Congress and the men who worked there, became head of the legislative department. Libby called her "brilliant, dynamic, and temperamental." But he, like Jeannette, liked to run things his own way, and so they clashed.

With Libby, Jeannette felt the sting of gender discrimination. Her political experience far surpassed the men in the organization, but Libby never treated her as an equal. He expected her to read

Frederick Libby founded the National Council for the Prevention of War and appointed Jeannette as the head of the legislative team. She worked with Libby for ten years.

Adolph Hitler, left, dictator of Germany under the Nazi regime, walks with Fascist Party leader Benito Mussolini, dictator of Italy. Together they plunged Europe and much of the world into World War II.

Military leaders in Japan seized political power and began a widespread invasion of the Far East. They invaded China in 1937. Street fighting in Shanghai is pictured here.

Jeannette visited Europe in 1937 and saw German fighter planes like these in the skies above her. It seemed to her as if war had already begun.

speeches that men had written, and paid her less than the men. Only her commitment to peace kept her working there. Finally, with the organization deep in debt, Libby cut her pay in half and she quit.

Meanwhile, as the 1930s progressed, Adolf Hitler and the Nazi Party seized power in Germany and Austria and began arming for war. Hitler ruled as a dictator and took away the freedoms of German citizens. Fascist leader Benito Mussolini took power in Italy and invaded Ethiopia. Italy and Germany gave military support during the Spanish Civil War to Francisco Franco, who became dictator of Spain. Japan built up a large army and invaded China.

President Franklin Roosevelt and the Congress had formed the New Deal during the 1930s, which created work for people who lost their jobs in the Great Depression. The government began social programs like Social Security, measures that the Progressives had supported twenty years before. Then, as the threat of war increased, Roosevelt tried to increase U.S. spending on the military. Many people resisted. They wanted to isolate themselves from another world war. Jeannette spoke before a congressional committee to urge the U.S. to remain neutral in case of war. Congress passed a one-year Neutrality Act in 1935 and renewed it in 1936, 1937, and 1939.

Jeannette traveled to Europe in 1931 and 1937 and was appalled by the military buildup in Italy and Germany. In Germany in 1937 she saw that "the planes were flying over and you would think that war was almost there." In 1939 war did break out in Europe when Nazi Germany attacked neighboring countries. The U.S. Congress agreed to send materials and money to the British to help them fight against Germany. Congress also vastly increased military spending in the United States and, in 1940, began drafting young men into the army. But still Roosevelt promised, "I have said this before, but I shall say it again and again and again; your boys are not going to be sent into any foreign wars."

Jeannette Rankin did not believe him. She had seen Roosevelt press for increased military spending since he became president in 1932. As the shadow of World War II crept across the world, she decided to run for Congress once more. She couldn't stop the war, but she wanted to keep the United States out of it. Congress was the best place to do that.

from **AN ARMISTICE DAY ARTICLE**

Let us not deceive ourselves. A war waged by the purest motives in the world does not change the essential attributes of war. Violence cannot contribute to the adjustment of human relationships, whether used individually or collectively by a nation or by a group of nations. War is still the stupid, futile method of attempting to settle disputes, regardless of who uses it or why.

Jeannette Rankin
written for the Associated Press
November 11, 1935

CHAPTER EIGHT

Back to Congress

When Jeannette Rankin ran for Congress again in 1940, she was sixty years old but as full of passion for political life as ever.

IN 1939 JEANNETTE MOVED FROM Georgia to Montana to run for Congress again. She began her campaign with high-school students. She called a school office to announce the day and time she was coming to speak. Then she hung up, without leaving her phone number. That way, the school couldn't call back to cancel, and when she showed up, they couldn't very well turn her away. She visited fifty-two of the fifty-six high schools in her congressional district.

"[T]he teachers were amazed that the children listened. But they listened," she said. "They listened if you talked sense to them. They'd listen if you treated them as if they had some intelligence." She talked about women's roles in politics. One day soon, she said, a woman will be president. When the boys groaned, she added that they would have new opportunities, too—as the president's husband!

She also explained why America should stay out of the war. The real threats to the country were unemployment and poverty. She would work to move America out of the Depression—and stay out of the war. Jeannette urged the students to write to their congressmen and tell them what they believed in. "You don't need to tell them how old you are. I never do!" she said.

Jeannette, at sixty, still had all her old energy and passion for politics. Many Montanans had forgotten about her. But now, teenagers brought her name to the dinner tables of ranchers, miners, and townspeople. They must have listened to their children, for Jeannette won the primary election against three Republican men in June 1940.

She traveled all over her western Montana district, stopping to speak to farmers, housewives, and other working people. Driving up a lonely canyon or walking the streets of towns and cities, she wanted to meet

After World War II began in Europe in 1939, the United States sent supplies to the Allies, Great Britain and France. To guard against attacks by German submarines, the ships traveled in convoys.

people, hear their views, and express her own. She sent voters copies of two of her radio speeches against war. This was her major campaign issue. "By voting for me … you can express your opposition to sending your son to foreign lands to fight in a foreign war." Most voters evidently agreed with her, for in November 1940 Jeannette won the election and became Congresswoman Rankin once again.

Back in Washington, Jeannette worked to prevent young American men from fighting overseas. Soon after Jeannette arrived in Congress, President Franklin Roosevelt proposed a law to allow him, without the consent of Congress, to send military supplies and information to Britain and its allies for the war against Germany and Japan.

Jeannette knew this Lend-Lease Act would bring the United States closer to war, but she decided to support the act if Congress would agree to amend it so that American soldiers wouldn't be sent to fight overseas. Congress rejected her amendment. A few months later she proposed the same amendment for another military bill, and again Congress rejected it. However, she was not alone. Over one-third of the Congress voted for both her amendments, and most Montanans supported her position.

Japanese planes bombed U.S. Navy ships at Pearl Harbor in Hawaii on December 7, 1941, killing and wounding more than three thousand people.

Jeannette spent most summers in Montana with her family. Here, in 1941, she stands in front of her brother Wellington's ranch house. Over the years, women's dresses got shorter and their hats got smaller.

Then on December 7, 1941, Japan attacked the U.S. naval forces in Pearl Harbor, Hawaii, destroying one-quarter of America's navy and killing and wounding more than three thousand people. The next day President Roosevelt planned to ask Congress to declare war.

Jeannette spent the morning driving around Washington, alone with her thoughts. "I got into my car and left the office. ... [N]o one knew where I was. And no one could get after me; no one could bring any pressure on me, because I knew what I was going to do."

After the president made his speech, the members of Congress began a debate. Several of them, who had opposed the war until now, described how Pearl Harbor had changed their minds. Passions ran high in the room.

Jeannette kept raising her hand to speak.

Speaker of the House Sam Rayburn, who controlled the discussion, ignored her.

She called out several times to get his attention, but he refused to call on her.

She stood up and said, "As a point of order, this has to go to the committee."

Still the Speaker ignored her.

Men shouted at her to sit down, and the Speaker ended the debate without letting her address the Congress.

The roll call began. When the clerk called

"Rankin," her voice rang out, "No! As a woman I cannot go to war, and I refuse to send anyone else." The vote was 388–1.

Fifty-five congressmen had joined her in opposing World War I in 1917. But now Jeannette Rankin stood alone. She was shouted down and booed. When the vote ended, angry people mobbed her. She managed to escape to a phone booth, where she called the congressional police, who escorted her to her office.

Later that day, she gave a statement to the press.

Sending our boys to the Orient [to fight Japan] will not protect this Country. We are all for every measure which will mean defense of our land, but taking our army and navy across thousands of miles of ocean to fight and die certainly cannot come under the heading of protecting our shores. ...

President Franklin D. Roosevelt asked Congress to declare war on Japan and its Axis partners, Germany and Italy, on December 8, 1941. Here he signs the declaration of war, officially beginning America's entry into World War II.

For months afterward she received vicious hate mail. Wellington said, "Montana is 110 percent against you." In the face of a brutal attack on the United States, her supporters had turned away from her. How did she feel? At the time, she said, "I have nothing left now except my integrity." Years later she added,

I was mad. ... Someone said, "Why do you have to vote against this?" I said, "Because I can't bear to be a worm." I was so mad. A hundred men ... that I had seen when I was lobbying, would say, "I'm just as much against war as you are." And I would answer that by saying, "Would you vote against a war resolution?" "I certainly would." And then they all forsook me.

Jeannette's vote against World War II was much more unpopular than her vote against World War I. U.S. territory in Hawaii had been attacked by Japan. People feared more air attacks on the West Coast. German submarines were spotted near the East Coast. Some Americans

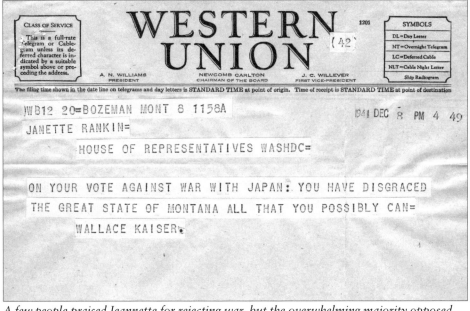

The filing time shown in the date line on telegrams and day letters is STANDARD TIME at point of origin. Time of receipt is STANDARD TIME at point of destination

WB12 20=BOZEMAN MONT 8 1158A   1941 DEC 8 PM 4 49

JANETTE RANKIN=

HOUSE OF REPRESENTATIVES WASHDC=

ON YOUR VOTE AGAINST WAR WITH JAPAN: YOU HAVE DISGRACED
THE GREAT STATE OF MONTANA ALL THAT YOU POSSIBLY CAN=

WALLACE KAISER.

A few people praised Jeannette for rejecting war, but the overwhelming majority opposed her. Some were vicious and threatening, others insulting and abusive. Here is one telegram she received.

Granted you are entitled to your own opinion. Thought [sic] heaven knows what alternative you have to offer to a nation that is already at war with us but at least you will have the honor of going down in the annals of history as the ultimate proof of the male contention that a womans [sic] place is in the home.
—Bess Meredyth

feared an invasion of enemy troops. Most people who wrote to Jeannette attacked her personally as well as politically.

One man said, "Having violated your oath as a member of the Congress in refusing to defend this nation from armed aggression, your action is an utter disgrace to the nation, and a humiliation to the people you represent. You can do a decent act by resigning from your office." The *Eugene* [Oregon] *Daily News* wrote, "Either Miss Rankin is stupid or emotionally unsound. In either case she does not belong in the House of Representatives."

But a few praised her courage, even as they disagreed with her vote. The editor of a pro-war newspaper, the *Emporia* [Kansas] *Gazette,* wrote:

Well—look at Jeannette Rankin. Probably a hundred men in

Congress would like to do what she did. Not one of them had the courage to do it.

The Gazette *entirely disagrees with the wisdom of her position. But, Lord, it was a brave thing: and its bravery somehow discounts its folly.*

The president of the American Civil Liberties Union wrote to Jeannette, "Integrity is a virtue in public life rare enough in a crisis to command admiration even among your opponents. You could only do what you did—and your act is heartening to all who cherish fidelity to principle and ideals." Jeannette's old friend Fiorello LaGuardia, quoting a popular song, wrote to her, "With all your faults I love you still."

Winston Churchill, prime minister of Great Britain during World War II, had wanted the United States to enter the war since it began in 1939. However, just six weeks before Jeannette cast her "no" vote, Churchill, speaking to schoolboys, said, "Never give in, never give in, never, never, never, never—in nothing, great or small, large or petty—never give in except to convictions of honour and good sense." Jeannette had followed his advice, but what would he have thought of her vote against entering the war?

Senator John F. Kennedy, who later became president, included Jeannette in his 1958 article in *McCall's Magazine* called "Three Women of Courage." He wrote,

Few members of Congress since its founding in 1789 have ever stood more alone, more completely in defiance of popular opinion,

Not everyone attacked Jeannette for her vote against World War II.

We always have causes for disputes, but we don't have to hit each other to settle them. We can run away with dignity or we can do something else. What they call "causes of war" are always lies. The real cause is that we have a military system that has to exist, and that military system creates disputes, and governments, in order to keep power, cause disputes.
Jeannette Rankin

U.S. troops land on an island in the Pacific Ocean. From early 1942 until mid-1945, over 16 million American troops fought in Europe and across the Pacific. Over 400,000 soldiers died and 670,000 were wounded.

Years of bombing by Allied and Axis powers left much of Europe in ruins. Here we see Nuremberg, Germany, at the end of the war.

than former Representative Jeannette Rankin of Montana. … Most of us do not associate the quality of courage with women in public affairs. We neither expect it nor reward it.

Jeannette Rankin was certainly not rewarded, but her courage kept her going as she fulfilled her duties as a congresswoman.

Most people see World War II as a clear case of right against wrong. They don't believe that America could or should have stayed out of the war against Nazi Germany and Imperial Japan. But Jeannette Rankin saw history differently. She saw how the world did nothing to preserve peace while Germany and Japan prepared for war. Jeannette said,

It isn't what the issues are, but the methods of settling disputes. … There's nothing you can do when you have war. War is wrong and everything that happens is wrong, and there's no way out. The only thing is to prevent *it. … I was just furious to think we hadn't stopped Hitler when it was possible to stop him.*

As long as they have war, I haven't anything to say because I have no way of making force and violence right. There's no way you can do it. The only way you can do it is to start at the bottom and create a new system of settling disputes and create it in the hearts of the people. The only thing is to start with children and people everywhere. We are all human beings and we have to live on this earth and we have to find a way of settling our disputes without force and violence.

Jeannette Rankin served out her second term in Congress, despite the hate mail that demanded her resignation. She had been given a job and she completed it as best she could. She tried to minimize the huge profits some corporations made during wartime. She voted to repeal the "Grab Act," which extended retirement benefits to the president and Congress, herself included. She believed that they should not have such benefits until all citizens did. She refused to take the extra gasoline ration she was allowed as a congresswoman.

Jeannette's mother had moved to Washington to live with her, and when Olive Rankin became ill, Jeannette spent a good deal of time nursing her. It was a difficult period for Jeannette. She knew that her political career was over, but she had followed her conscience, whatever the price.

WORLD WAR II

Following a severe economic depression in the 1920s, many—but not all—Germans believed Adolph Hitler's propaganda that Germany could become the most powerful nation on earth. In 1933 Hitler became chancellor of Germany and set up a dictatorship. He took away the civil rights of all Germans and began a campaign of hate, especially against Jews. He built a powerful army and in 1938 began invading nearby countries. In 1939 Great Britain and France declared war against Germany, and the Nazi Army soon conquered nearly all of Western Europe. Only Britain remained free. Italy, under the Fascist dictator Benito Mussolini, joined Germany and Japan to form the Axis powers.

Japan invaded China in 1937 and began a military conquest of Asia. Many Americans, though they sympathized with the victims of Japanese and German aggression, wanted to stay out of the war. Then on December 7, 1941, Japanese airplanes attacked Hawaii. Nearly all Americans then supported the war.

By 1945, when World War II ended with the surrender of Germany and Japan, more than sixty million people had died. Nine million died in Nazi concentration camps, including six million Jews. The United States dropped two atomic bombs on Japanese cities, killing two hundred thousand civilians and poisoning many more. The level of destruction of World War II and the threat of nuclear weapons produced fear and dread of a possible World War III.

The United States dropped an atomic bomb on Hiroshima, Japan, on August 6, 1945. Seventy thousand people died instantly. More than thirty thousand died later of injuries and radiation poisoning. Three days later the U.S. dropped another atomic bomb on Nagasaki. Japan then surrendered and World War II ended.

CHAPTER NINE

A Leader Once Again

Jeannette Rankin sits on horseback at her brother Wellington's ranch in Montana, 1952. After her second term in Congress, Jeannette divided her time between Montana, her small house in Georgia, and her travels around the world.

WHEN JEANNETTE LEFT CONGRESS IN 1943, SHE HAD NO HOPE of reelection. She returned to Montana to care for her invalid mother. Her sisters Grace and Edna shared this difficult task, but Jeannette remained the main caregiver. In 1945 World War II ended when Germany and Japan surrendered. No one listened to Jeannette's peace message now, so she retreated to private life.

She had long admired Mahatma Gandhi's nonviolent campaign to persuade Great Britain to grant independence to India. For thirty years the British-trained lawyer had worked for self-government for the Indian people, always insisting on nonviolence. Gandhi and his followers used writings, meetings, demonstrations, boycotts, and marches to achieve their goal. They finally succeeded in 1947. Jeannette described her admiration this way, "Gandhi said, 'Resist evil. Resist it with your life if necessary, but resist with nonviolence.'" How like Jeannette's own philosophy!

Mahatma Gandhi, right, led the Indian people to independence from Great Britain by nonviolent actions. Here he sits with Jawaharlal Nehru, who became the first prime minister of a free, democratic India.

She set sail for India in 1946. Gandhi was assassinated before she could meet him, but she did meet the first Indian prime minister, Jawaharlal Nehru. Nehru, along with many others, had spent years in prison for nonviolent activities. Nehru spoke to Jeannette with glowing praise about his wife and other women who worked for Indian independence, even going to prison for their principles.

Jeannette Rankin explored Gandhi's legacy of nonviolence during her seven trips to India, sometimes traveling over rough roads in an old Ford that she shipped from America. Gandhi believed in returning to a simple rural life—like Jeannette had done in Georgia. More importantly, he believed that group actions such as protest marches, boycotts, and strikes could peaceably bring about political change. In the 1950s and 1960s, Dr. Martin Luther King Jr. brought these techniques to the United States civil rights movement.

Jeannette also traveled to Asia, Europe, Africa, and Latin America to study other cultures. She found

At an age when most people retire, Jeannette began to travel the world. She loved to meet people wherever she went. Here in Japan, she visits with a group of schoolboys. Women's hats became smaller over the decades, but Jeannette still wore one.

In Egypt Jeannette rode a camel at the Pyramids and sent this picture to her brother.

Jeannette's first house in Georgia, with its groves of pecan trees, burned down in the early 1940s. She bought another old farmhouse, shown here.

friendship everywhere she went, and when people learned of her political past, they asked her to give speeches. "I wasn't idle," she said.

In exchange for caring for their mother, who died in 1947 at age ninety-three, Wellington supported Jeannette for the rest of her life. He was one of the richest men in Montana and he gave generously to his sisters and their children. He never had any children of his own. For Jeannette, he bought a ranch and ran it for her. He gave her investments that brought her a monthly income, bought her cars, and paid for some of her travels.

Her house in Georgia had burned down during her second term in Congress, so she bought another farm nearby. She lived in a little shack and built a bigger house for a local family. Wonder Robinson and his wife, Mattie, helped Jeannette over the years. Their children, Stanley, Jeff, and Jennifer, became like grandchildren to her. She gave Wonder and Mattie their house and land in her will, and left money for the children.

As the years passed, few of Jeannette's friends came to visit her in Georgia. They were growing older. Jeannette didn't slow down, though. Her friends begged her to come and see them, but she never seemed to visit as often or stay as long as they wanted. Jeannette had her moments of loneliness. She could have settled down with any one of several close friends, but she didn't. In her seventies, on a trip to India, she met an American doctor sixteen years younger than herself. Back in the United States, he wrote, inviting her to be his "dear companion … to share what remains of life and love." But, just as she had done fifty years earlier with her boyfriends in Montana, Jeannette chose her independence.

As she traveled the world, her curiosity roamed freely as well.

As a girl, Jeannette had examined her father's farm machines to see how they worked. Now, she studied governments and world affairs for the same reason. She believed that democracy, equal rights, and social justice laid the foundation for peace. She looked at the U.S. government to see how it could provide such a foundation. She

Jeannette built a house on her Georgia property for Wonder and Mattie Robinson and made friends with their children, Stanley, Jennifer, and Jeff Robinson, above. The Robinsons helped Jeannette with housework and chores.

liked what she saw in the Supreme Court—a peaceful system of settling disputes.

> *[W]e should ... try to understand why the Supreme Court can function as it does—nonviolently and without an instrument of coercion. Its decisions are followed because of respect for the idea of law and the common good. The Supreme Court is a human institution. It can change its mind. But the reason it is obeyed is because it settles disputes ... nonviolently: people understand that a settlement through law and courts may be against the short-term interests of one party, but both parties maintain life and often liberty and the opportunity to pursue happiness—but the settlement brought by violence is the settlement of death, and all the issues are mooted [irrelevant.] War and bloodshed settle nothing happily.*

"Respect for the idea of law and the common good" formed the basis of her work in the suffrage movement, Congress, and the peace movement. She had tried to translate the "common good" into the laws of the land.

Jeannette Rankin didn't make the news anymore. When she wasn't traveling, she spent summers in Montana and the rest of the year in

For over forty years following World War II, the United States and the Soviet Union built up enormous military forces, armed with enough nuclear weapons to destroy each other and all countries in between. Historians called this the Cold War. In this 1961 political cartoon, U.S. president John F. Kennedy and Soviet premier Nikita Khrushchev stand in quicksand, glaring at each other.

Jeannette stayed out of the newspapers after her second term in Congress. But her native Montanans didn't forget her. In August 1961 she was given an honorary degree of Doctor of Laws from Montana State College at Bozeman.

Georgia, far from the centers of political power.

After World War II and throughout the 1950s, America prospered. Many women who had worked in offices and factories while men fought in the war went home again to keep house and raise children. The United States and the Soviet Union became military superpowers, each with huge stockpiles of nuclear weapons.

Social concerns in the United States spurred a few people to action. During the 1950s, Dr. Martin Luther King Jr. began a nonviolent campaign for African American civil rights. Pacifists formed the Committee for a Sane Nuclear Policy. Both these movements were small at first but would grow in the years to come.

In the early 1960s the United States sent 15,000 troops to South Vietnam to help fight communist forces from North Vietnam. The United States feared the spread of communism in Southeast Asia. The government believed that if the North Vietnamese conquered South Vietnam, they could attack neighboring countries. For this reason, the U.S. government and many Americans (64 percent in 1965) supported the war. Many Americans, but not all.

Jeannette Rankin began to speak out once more. She sent antiwar ads to newspapers, but they often refused to print them. She addressed a class of college students and was not invited back. She tried to speak on Atlanta public television but was rejected. Half of the United States budget went for military expenses, and she refused to pay some of her taxes, calling them "war taxes." But the government took the money from her bank account.

A few years later, in the late 1960s, 500,000 American soldiers were fighting in Southeast Asia. According to the U.S. Constitution, only Congress has the power to declare war, as it had done, despite Jeannette Rankin's "no" votes in 1917 and 1941. But Congress never voted to declare war in Vietnam. Instead, in 1964 Congress passed the Gulf of Tonkin Resolution, which gave President Lyndon Johnson power "to take all necessary measures to repel any armed attack against the forces of the United States and to prevent further aggression." Under this resolution—which had no expiration date—Congress voted to fund the Vietnam War for nine more years, until a peace treaty was signed in 1973.

As the war expanded, more and more Americans opposed it (61 percent in 1971). College students organized the first protests, but eventually people of all ages and political opinions joined in. They marched, wrote articles and spoke out, organized sit-in demonstrations and teach-ins on campuses.

Some protesters were pacifists who opposed all wars. Others opposed this particular war. They claimed it was a Vietnamese conflict and the United States shouldn't intervene. Still others saw it as a losing cause and wanted to withdraw to prevent further bloodshed. Some young men refused to be drafted into the army

MISS JEANNETTE RANKIN
CITATION

In recognition of the breadth of vision which enabled you to sense major developments in this century, and your untiring efforts to further their progress; for your leadership in the woman suffrage movement and your consequent election as the first woman in the world to serve in a major legislative body; for your dignified and effective conduct of that office which advanced the status of women in public life; for the courage of your conviction that international differences should be settled by mediation rather than by force; for your continuing concern that the underprivileged groups at home and in the underdeveloped countries abroad share in economic and social progress which will promote peace throughout the world;

I have the honor to confer upon you by virtue of the authority vested in me by the State Board of Education, ex officio Regents of the University of Montana, by law, and on the recommendation of the faculty of Montana State College, the Honorary Degree of Doctor of Laws.

Roland R. Renne, President

U.S. and South Vietnamese troops force women and children, perhaps suspected of enemy activity, out of their village. Americans watched scenes like this each night on television news. The war in Vietnam was the longest war in American history, from the early 1960s to 1975.

and went to jail or fled to Canada. Returning soldiers formed Vietnam Veterans Against the War. Eventually some soldiers fighting in Vietnam published antiwar newsletters, refused to obey orders, and deserted in large numbers.

Amid this growing throng of people who opposed the Vietnam War stood Jeannette Rankin, now in her eighties. April 1967 was the fiftieth anniversary of Jeannette's vote against World War I in Congress, and newspaper reporters wrote about her. Then a peace group in Atlanta asked her to speak and the story was reported across the country. Jeannette's message hadn't changed.

It isn't a question of war against Germany, Japan, or Vietnam. It's just that the whole system is very stupid. … Shooting a young man is no way to settle a political dispute. You cannot change opinion by force.

We drifted into this Vietnam War and we can drift out.

How can we get our boys home? Why the same way we got them over there, by planes and ships.

In 1917, when Jeannette voted against World War I, her brother said, "You know you're not going to get re-elected." She answered, "I'm not interested in that. All I'm interested in is what they will say fifty years from now." Fifty years later, in 1967, people were heaping praise on her. The feminists and the peace movement "discovered" Jeannette Rankin. Many had never heard of her. Others thought she had died. But she was very much alive. Some people viewed her as a curious antique from the past. She refused to play that role. She didn't dwell on her past accomplishments. Instead, she focused on present circumstances.

She challenged women to act against the Vietnam War. "We—women—should picket everything. This is no time to be polite." Ten thousand U.S. soldiers had died in Vietnam by mid-1967 when Jeannette planned her march. If ten thousand women marched on Washington, she said, they could end the war.

On January 15, 1968, thousands of women gathered in Washington, D.C., to march through the streets to Congress. They called themselves the Jeannette Rankin Brigade. Jeannette, as opinionated

Jeannette Rankin, along with her sister Edna and niece Dorothy, met with Montana senator Mike Mansfield at the end of the Jeannette Rankin Peace March in January 1968. Rankin and Mansfield were old friends, and his was a strong antiwar voice in the U.S. Senate.

as ever at eighty-seven years old, didn't like the military name *brigade.* Yet she was in the front row, marching with Coretta Scott King, wife of Dr. Martin Luther King Jr.; Black Panther Bobbie Hodges; several senators' wives; and five thousand other women, some pushing strollers or carrying babies on their backs. Their banner demanded that the U.S. government "End the War in Vietnam and Social Crisis at Home!"

When they reached the Capitol, Jeannette Rankin refused a policeman's offer to help her up the stairs. She went to see Senator Mike Mansfield from Montana, who had taken over her seat in Congress when she left in 1943. He tried to offer her a cup of tea, but this was not a social call. Jeannette wanted to talk about ending the war. Senator Mansfield was a strong opponent of the war, so Jeannette simply told him to bring "the boys" home from Vietnam *now.*

This was not Jeannette's first protest march and it would not be her last. She had marched for women's suffrage in Washington in 1913. She had marched for peace in Chicago in 1932. Then, for many years, she walked alone. Now, at last, she found people to march with her again.

More and more women were entering politics. Jeannette had led the way in 1916. Hippies moved to the country to live simply. Jeannette had lived like that since 1924. Americans of all ages said no to the Vietnam

Petition of the Jeannette Rankin Brigade presented to Congress in January 1968

We, Women of the United States, who are outraged by the ruthless slaughter in Vietnam and the persistent neglect of human needs at home, have come to Washington to petition the Congress of the United States for the redress of intolerable grievances and demand that:

1) Congress shall, as the first order of business, resolve to end the war in Vietnam and immediately withdraw all American troops.

2) Congress shall use its power to heal a sick society at home.

3) Congress shall use its power to make reparations for the ravaged land we leave behind in Vietnam.

4) Congress shall listen to what the American people are saying and refuse the insatiable demands of the military industrial complex.

War. Jeannette had said no to two world wars. People had come around to her way of thinking, and she just laughed and said, "Can you imagine? I'm respectable!"

For the next few years she continued to march against the Vietnam War and speak out for government reform and social justice. She campaigned for the direct election of presidents, not the convoluted Electoral College system that the country still has. She wanted multimember congressional districts, like Montana had had when she was elected to Congress in 1916. She believed that one congressperson cannot represent all the people in a district. Give people more options. Let them choose more than one representative.

Jeannette traveled by airplane, not horse and buggy. She spoke on television, not on street corners. Historians interviewed her for biographies and oral history projects. She told them, "I worked ten years for suffrage and got it. I have worked fifty-six years for peace and have hardly begun."

Awards and honors came her way when she turned ninety in 1970. Fifteen hundred people stood and applauded when she became the first member of the Susan B. Anthony Hall of Fame in 1972. They called her "the world's outstanding living feminist." Jeannette claimed, only half-joking, that she considered running for Congress again, "just to have someone to vote for!" She died the following year in her sleep, peacefully.

Jeannette Rankin didn't achieve her goals—peace, equal opportunity for women, social justice for all—but she never lost hope and she never quit trying. She praised what was best in her society and worked to make it better.

In her Montana childhood she learned that even if you were stubborn, you worked alongside your family. During her suffrage days, she insisted on forming local suffrage groups, not giving self-serving speeches. In Congress she worked with her colleagues, even when they opposed her. Jeannette believed in democracy and she believed in people. "Progress can only come from the masses," she said.

At the end of her long life, someone asked Jeannette Rankin what advice she had for young people, and she answered with one word: "Organize."

In 1910 Jeannette Rankin spoke in dance halls about women's suffrage. Sixty years later in 1970, when she was ninety years old, she spoke out at this rock concert and antiwar rally at the University of Georgia.

Women must devote all their energies today in gaining enough political offices to influence the direction of government away from the military-industrial complex and toward solving the major social disgraces that exist in our country.

Jeannette Rankin
Susan B. Anthony Hall of Fame
Award Presentation, 1972

TIMELINE

1880   June 11: JR born in Grant Creek, Montana.

1883   The railroad comes to Missoula, Montana.

1889   Montana becomes the 41st state.

1893   New Zealand grants women the right to vote.

1898   JR enters Montana State University in Missoula.

1902   JR graduates with a degree in biology.

1904–05 JR visits her brother, Wellington, in Boston; travels to New York City and Washington, D.C.

1906   Finland becomes the first European country to give women the right to vote.

1907   JR visits San Francisco; works in a settlement house.

1908   JR enters the New York School of Philanthropy; graduates in 1909.

1909   JR works at Children's Home Society in Washington State.

1910   JR studies at the University of Washington, Seattle; volunteers for Washington State suffrage campaign; November: women win the vote in Washington State.

1911   February 1: JR speaks to Montana legislature on women's suffrage.

1911–14 JR campaigns across the U.S. for National American Woman Suffrage Association.

1913   March 3: Women's suffrage parade of 5,000 held in Washington, D.C.; Jeannette marches for Montana.

1914   JR returns to Montana for women's suffrage campaign; travels 9,000 miles speaking and organizing; November 3: women's suffrage passes.

1914   August: World War I declared in Europe.

1915   JR travels to New Zealand.

1916   JR returns to Montana; runs for Congress on Republican ticket; November 6: elected the first U.S. congresswoman.

1917   April 2: JR enters Congress; President Woodrow Wilson asks for declaration of war to enter World War I; April 6: JR votes against the war.

TIMELINE

1918   November: JR loses election to the U.S. Senate; Germany surrenders; World War I ends.

1919   JR travels to Switzerland for International Congress of Women for Permanent Peace; visits war-torn France; Treaty of Versailles punishes Germany harshly.

1920   Nineteenth Amendment to the Constitution becomes law, giving U.S. women the vote.

1920–24 JR lobbies for labor and family issues.

1922   Fascist Party leader Benito Mussolini becomes dictator of Italy.

1924   JR buys farm in Georgia.

1924–39 JR works for peace groups, traveling and speaking, as well as lobbying in Washington, D.C.

1929   New York Stock Market crash triggers the Great Depression, lasting until World War II.

1932   JR leads peace march from Washington, D.C., to Chicago.

1933   Nazi Party leader Adolph Hitler becomes dictator of Germany.

1934   American Legion attacks proposed Brenau College Chair of Peace for JR.

1934–37 JR works with Senator Gerald Nye on investigation of WWI war profits and on Neutrality Acts to keep U.S. out of war.

1935   JR sues *Macon Evening News* for libel after the newspaper called her a communist.

1936   Newspaper settles JR's lawsuit and prints a retraction.

1937   Japan invades China; JR visits Germany and sees military buildup.

1939   World War II begins: Germany invades Poland; Great Britain and France declare war.

1940   JR runs for Congress in Montana on a peace platform; wins November election.

1941   December 7: Japan attacks Pearl Harbor; December 8: President Franklin D. Roosevelt asks Congress for declaration of war; JR casts the only vote against the war.

1943   JR returns to Montana when her term in Congress ends.

TIMELINE

1945   May 7: Germany surrenders, ending the war in Europe; August 6: U.S. drops an atomic bomb on Hiroshima, Japan; August 9: U.S. drops an atomic bomb on Nagasaki, Japan; Japan surrenders on August 14; World War II ends.

1946–70   JR travels to India seven times and to Asia, Africa, Europe, and Latin America.

1947   India gains independence from Great Britain.

1948   Mahatma Gandhi assassinated by Hindu extremist.

1961   President John F. Kennedy sends military advisers to Vietnam to assist South Vietnamese Army against North Vietnam.

1961   JR awarded Doctor of Laws honorary degree from Montana State College.

1964   August: U.S. begins bombing North Vietnam; Congress approves Gulf of Tonkin Resolution, which gives President Johnson power to wage undeclared war.

1965   U.S. combat troops sent to Vietnam; antiwar demonstrations held all across U.S.

1968   January 15: Jeannette Rankin Brigade of 5,000 women protest the Vietnam War.

1968–73   JR speaks out against the war at colleges, rallies, and on television.

1970   June 11: JR's 90th birthday party held in Washington, D.C.; honored by past and present politicians.

1972   JR becomes the first member of the Susan B. Anthony Hall of Fame.

1973   January 27: Peace treaty signed, ending U.S. involvement in the Vietnam War; May 18: JR dies peacefully in Carmel, California.

SELECTED BIBLIOGRAPHY

BOOKS FOR ADULTS

Giles, Kevin S. *Flight of the Dove: The Story of Jeannette Rankin*. Beaverton,
OR: Touchstone Press, 1980.

Harris, Ted C. *Jeannette Rankin: Suffragist, First Woman Elected to Congress, and Pacifist*.
New York: Arno Press, 1982.

Josephson, Hannah. *Jeannette Rankin, First Lady in Congress: A Biography*.
Indianapolis: Bobbs-Merrill, 1974.

Lopach, James J., and Jean A. Luckowski. *Jeannette Rankin: A Political Woman*.
Boulder: University Press of Colorado, 2005.

Smith, Norma. *Jeannette Rankin: America's Conscience*.
Helena: Montana Historical Society Press, 2002.

ARTICLES FOR ADULTS

All Things Considered. National Public Radio, December 7, 2001.

Anthony, Katharine. "A Basket of Summer Fruit." *Woman's Home Companion*,
August 1926, 11–12, 50, 52.

——— "Living on the Front Porch." *Woman's Home Companion*,
September 1926, 32, 34, 83–84.

Kennedy, John F. "Three Women of Courage." *McCall's Magazine*,
January 1958, 36–37, 54–55.

The Ladies' Home Journal. "What is Coming Out of the War That is Touching
the American Woman: An Editorial." February 1915, 3.

The Jeannette Rankin Papers at the Schlesinger Library on the History of Women in
America, Radcliffe Institute, Cambridge, Massachusetts, contain a large collection of
newspaper clippings, official and personal letters, speeches, etc.

Additional materials on Jeannette Rankin held by the Montana Historical Society, Helena,
Montana.

BOOKS FOR CHILDREN AND YOUNG ADULTS

Biographies

Davidson, Sue. *A Heart in Politics: Jeannette Rankin and Patsy T. Mink*.
Seattle: Seal Press, 1994.

Marx, Trish. *Jeannette Rankin: First Lady of Congress*.
New York: Margaret K. McElderry Books, 2006.

O'Brien, Mary Barmeyer. *Jeannette Rankin, 1880–1973: Bright Star in the Big Sky*.
Helena, MT: Falcon Press, 1995.

SELECTED BIBLIOGRAPHY

Anthologies

Fireside, Bryna J. *Is There a Woman in the House—or Senate?*
Morton Grove, IL: A. Whitman, 1994.

Krull, Kathleen. *Lives of Extraordinary Women: Rulers, Rebels (and What the Neighbors Thought).* San Diego: Harcourt, 2000.

History

Ambrose, Stephen E. *The Good Fight: How World War II Was Won.*
New York: Atheneum, 2001.

Bausum, Ann. *With Courage and Cloth: Winning the Fight for a Woman's Right to Vote.*
Washington, DC: National Geographic, 2004.

Caputo, Philip. *10,000 Days of Thunder: A History of the Vietnam War.*
New York: Atheneum, 2005.

Dolan, Edward F. *America in World War I.* Brookfield, CT: Millbrook Press, 1996.

George, Linda S. *WWI: Letters from the Homefront.*
New York: Benchmark Books, 2002.

Meltzer, Milton. *Ain't Gonna Study War No More: The Story of America's Peace Seekers.*
New York: Random House, 2002.

Schomp, Virginia. *The Vietnam War: Letters from the Battlefront.*
New York: Benchmark Books, 2002.

——*World War II: Letters from the Battlefront.* New York: Benchmark Books, 2002.

WEB SITES*

The Architect of the Capitol. www.aoc.gov/cc/art/nsh/rankin.cfm.
Describes the statue of Jeannette Rankin in the U.S. Capitol.

The Jeannette Rankin Foundation. www.rankinfoundation.org/. Awards scholarships to women over thirty-five.

The Jeannette Rankin Peace Center. www.jrpc.org. The center's mission is "to connect and empower people to build a socially just, non-violent, and sustainable world."

National Women's Hall of Fame.
www.greatwomen.org/women.php?action=viewone&id=121. Features a short biography of Jeannette Rankin.

Nuclear Age Peace Foundation.
www.wagingpeace.org/menu/programs/youth-outreach/peace-heroes/rankin-jeannette/htm.
Jeannette Rankin is one of the foundation's "peace heroes."

Rankin, Jeannette. "Activist for World Peace, Women's Rights, and Democratic Government." Typescript of an oral history conducted in 1972 by Malca Chall and Hannah Josephson. Regional Oral History Office, The Bancroft Library, University of California, Berkeley. 293 pp. Online at the California Digital Library, http://ark.cdlib.org/ark:/13030/kt758005dx/.

*Active at the time of publication

SOURCE NOTES

The source of each quotation is found in the following notes. The citation indicates the first words of a quotation and its document source.

CHAPTER ONE: **Still Marching** page 11

"I don't know ...": Smith, p. 27.
"You don't need to worry ...": Josephson, p. 188.
"To All American Women": Schlesinger Library, Jeannette Rankin Papers.
"The work of educating ...": Smith, p. 158.
"We haven't taken care ...": California Digital Library, p. 150.

CHAPTER TWO: **Growing Up in Montana** page 14

"If you can take care ...": Smith, p. 34.
"You could almost see ...": California Digital Library, p. 288.
"I was a very poor student ...": California Digital Library, p. 282.
"When I was in school ...": California Digital Library, p. 240.
"You haven't sense enough ...": California Digital Library, p. 189.
"it was just the thing ...": Smith, p. 41.
"Half a league ...": Alfred, Lord Tennyson, *The Poetic and Dramatic Works of Alfred Lord Tennyson* (Cambridge, MA: Houghton Mifflin, 1898), pp. 226–227.
"This is hideous ...": Harris, p. 28.
"Go! Go! Remember ...": Smith, p. 46 [picture caption].

CHAPTER THREE: **The Making of a Progressive** page 22

"That's just Jeannette ...": Smith, p. 53.
"There wasn't enough money ...": Smith, p. 55.
"the poster in his window ...": Smith, p. 56.
"the only place ...": California Digital Library, p. 47.
"Your ... representative ...": Smith, p. 62.
"You men of the West ...": Smith, p. 63.
"It's a woman's place ...": Smith, p. 63.
"I was always taught ...": California Digital Library, p. 237.
"At first I thought ...": California Digital Library, p. 154.

CHAPTER FOUR: **Back Home to Montana** page 30

"I was born in Montana!": Smith, p. 78.
"We are not asking ...": *Helena Independent*, February 2, 1911.
"To Miss Jeannette ...": *Helena Independent*, February 2, 1911.
"The female vote ...": Francis Parkman, *Some of the Reasons Against Woman Suffrage* (Boston: Printed at the request of an Association of Women, 1884), p. 4.
"In politics I do not ...": *Harper's Bazaar,* May 19, 1894, p. 1.
"I took it for granted ...": Eleanor Roosevelt, *This Is My Story.* (New York: Harper and Brothers, 1937), pp. 180–181.
"Women in our organization ...": Smith, p. 82.

SOURCE NOTES

"Never mind if you ...": Smith, p. 94.
"Jeannette Rankin is ...": *Women's Journal XLV,* March 7, 1914, quoted in Harris, p. 80.
"I want my ...": Harris, p. 89.
"STOP LOOK LISTEN ...": Smith, p. 84.
"Suffrage Song ...": Pamphlet Collection, Mansfield Library, University of Montana, Missoula.

CHAPTER FIVE: **The Road to Congress**   page 40

"I had very little money ...": Smith, p. 97.
"If they are going to ...": Smith, p. 101.
"I told the eastern women ...": Smith, pp. 98–99.
"I'll manage your ...": Wellington Rankin, interview by V. W. Steele, Montana Historical
    Society, Helena, undated.
"I never was ...": California Digital Library, p. 60.
"There are hundreds of men ...": Smith, p. 102.
"He kept us out ...": Meltzer, p. 139.
"I knew the women ...": *Detroit Free Press,* November 11, 1916.
"Her life is devoted ...": Giles, p. 83.
"Jeannette will make ...": Harris, p. 107.
"I'm not nervous ...": *Seattle Sunday Times,* November 26, 1916.
"Women ought to have ...": Josephson, p. 65.
"There will be many times ...": *Daily Missoulian* (Missoula, Montana), April 7, 1917.
"BRASS BANDS GREET ...": *Kalispell Times* (Kalispell, Montana), August 17, 1916.
"What I Expect to Do ...": Jeannette Rankin, *New York Sunday American,* November 26, 1916.
"The Congresslady ...": Christopher Morley, *New York Times Sunday Magazine,*
    November 19, 1916.

CHAPTER SIX: **"I Cannot Vote for War."**   page 48

"Not more than ...": Smith, p. 110.
"The world must be made ...": *Congressional Record,* LV, pt. 1, April 2, 1917, p. 120.
"the United States ...": *Congressional Record,* August, 20, 1914, pp. 140–142.
"[L]et me at once remind ...": *Congressional Record,* LV, April 5, 1917, p. 332.
"if I could see any ...": Smith, p. 111.
"I want to stand ...": *Daily Missoulian* (Missoula, Montana), April 6, 1917.
"Miss Rankin was not voting ...": *New York Times,* April 7, 1914.
"Our Congress Lady ...": Smith, p. 113.
"She would consider ...": Wellington Rankin, interview by V. W. Steele, Montana Historical
    Society, Helena, undated.
"I knew it would be ...": California Digital Library, p. 154.
"We did not labor ...": California Digital Library, p. 155.
"I believe that the first ...": Josephson, p. 78.
"I think I know ...": *Rocky Mountain News* (Denver, Colorado), August 9, 1917.
"The great army of labor ...": Smith, p. 117.
"It is time for our old ...": *Congressional Record,* LVI, pp. 771–772.
"I have always regretted ...": Lopach and Luckowski, pp. 139–140.
"Am bending every effort ...": Lopach and Luckowski, p. 140.
"In 1917 [the House] ...": California Digital Library, pp. 256–257.

SOURCE NOTES

"The number of ...": *Bridgeport Telegram*, July 18, 1917.
"Before World War I ...": California Digital Library, p. 178.

CHAPTER SEVEN: **Fighting for Peace**   page 58

"Miss Addams was ...": California Digital Library, pp. 199–200.
"She was a perfect ...": Smith, p. 149.
"Your message appeals ...": Carrie A. Foster, *The Women and the Warriors*
     (Syracuse, NY: Syracuse University Press, 1995), p. 30.
"[O]pen the channels ...": California Digital Library, p. 186.
"This International Congress ...": Gertrude Bussey and Margaret Tims, *Women's
     International League for Peace and Freedom* (London: Allen and Unwin, 1965), p. 31.
"The right of citizens ...": U.S. Constitution.
"It was women's work ...": Harris, p. 85.
"the chief business ...": Calvin Coolidge (speech, American Society of Newspaper Editors,
     January 17, 1925), www.asne.org.
"I felt very sorry ...": Josephson, p. 115.
"[Jeannette] always had guests ...": Katharine Anthony, "A Basket of Summer Fruit,"
     Woman's Home Companion, August 1926, p. 12.
"[Jeannette] cherished her trees ...": same as above, p. 11.
"You don't know how hard ...": Smith, p. 156.
"From our front window ...": Lopach and Luckowski, p. 39.
"We have over ...": Lopach and Luckowski, pp. 39–40.
"I ... said you had to organize ...": California Digital Library, p. 14.
"Just stubborn ...": Smith, p. 27.
"detrimental to the welfare ...": Harris, pp. 222–223.
"We say welcome ...": Giles, p. 144.
"The sum of my ...": Giles, p. 144.
"brilliant, dynamic, and temperamental": Smith, p. 160.
"the planes were flying over ...": Harris, p. 266.
"I have said this before ...": The National Archives,
     www.archives.gov/education/lessons/fdr-churchill.
"It is not patriotism ...": *Atlanta Georgian*, October 13, 1934.
"Let us not deceive ...": Jeannette Rankin, "An Armistice Day Article,"
     Associated Press, November 11, 1935.

CHAPTER EIGHT: **Back to Congress**   page 72

"[T]he teachers were amazed ...": California Digital Library, p. 242.
"You don't need to ...": California Digital Library, p. 66.
"By voting for me ...": *Congressional Record Appendix*, 76th Congress, 3rd session,
     August 7, 1940, p. 4837.
"I got into my car ...": California Digital Library, p. 10.
"As a point of order ...": National Public Radio, transcript of Congressional debate,
     December 8, 1941.
"No! As a woman ...": Josephson, p. 162.
"Sending our boys ...": Smith, p. 184.

SOURCE NOTES

"Montana is 110 ...": Smith, p. 184.

"I have nothing ...": Smith, p. 184.

"I was mad ...": California Digital Library, pp. 214–215.

"Having violated your oath ...": Schlesinger Library, Jeannette Rankin Papers.

"Either Miss Rankin ...": *Eugene Daily News* (Eugene, Oregon), December 1941.

"Well—look at Jeannette ...": *Emporia Gazette* (Emporia, Kansas), December 10, 1941.

"Integrity is a virtue ...": Smith, p. 185.

"With all your faults ...": Smith, p. 185.

"Never give in, never ...": Winston Churchill (speech, Harrow School, October 29, 1941),
    The Churchill Centre, www.winstonchurchill.org.

"Few members of Congress ...": John F. Kennedy, "Three Women of Courage,"
    McCall's Magazine, January 1958, p. 37.

"It isn't what the issues ...": California Digital Library, pp. 276–277.

"Granted you are ...": Schlesinger Library, Jeannette Rankin Papers.

"We always have causes ...": California Digital Library, p. 278.

CHAPTER NINE: **A Leader Once Again**   page 80

"Gandhi said, 'Resist ...'": Lopach and Luckowski, p. 186.

"I wasn't idle.": California Digital Library, p. 12.

"dear companion ...": Lopach and Luckowski, p. 48.

"[W]e should ... try to understand ...": California Digital Library, p. 107.

"to take all necessary ...": Gulf of Tonkin Resolution, Public Law 88-408, 88th Congress,
    (August 7, 1964), General Records of the United States Government.

"Miss Jeannette Rankin": Schlesinger Library, Jeannette Rankin Papers.

"It isn't a question ...": Smith, p. 209.

"You know you're not ...": Wellington Rankin, interview by V. W. Steele,
    Montana Historical Society, Helena, undated.

"We—women—should picket ...": Smith, p. 209.

"Petition of the Jeannette ...": *Washington Post*, January 16, 1968.

"Can you imagine? ...": Smith, p. 210.

"I worked ten years ...": California Digital Library, p. 115.

"the world's outstanding ...": Smith, p. 221.

"just to have someone ...": California Digital Library, p. 172.

"Progress can only ...": California Digital Library, p. 181.

"Organize.": California Digital Library, p. 152.

"Women must devote all ...": Josephson, p. 204.

PICTURE SOURCES

Brenau University Archives Photo Collection: 68

NY School of Philanthropy Class of 1908-09–Group Photo; Columbia University Archives; **Columbia University in the City of New York**: 25 (bottom)

Corbis: 11

What is Coming Out of the War That is Touching the American Woman, Ladies' Home Journal Editorial, Copyright February 1915, Reprinted with the permission of **LADIES' HOME JOURNAL**, Meredith Corporation: 57

Library of Congress Prints and Photographs Division, LC-USZ62-231: 22; Library of Congress Prints and Photographs Division, LC-USZ62-63966: 23; Library of Congress Prints and Photographs Division, LC-USZ62-71202: 25 (top); Library of Congress Prints and Photographs Division, LC-USZ62-20570: 33; Library of Congress, LC-USZ62-95606: 34 (bottom left); Library of Congress Prints and Photographs Division, LC-USZ62-22262: 34 (top right); Library of Congress Prints and Photographs Division, LC-USZC4-2996: 34 (top left); Library of Congress Newspaper and Periodicals Reading Room, LC-DIG-ppmsca-02946: 35; Library of Congress, Prints and Photographs Division, LC-USZ62-28475: 36; Library of Congress, LC-USZ62-95344: 37 (top left); Library of Congress, LC-USZ62-112685, George Grantham Bain Collection: 40; Library of Congress, LC-USZ62-92808, Photo by International News Photos, Inc.: 49; Library of Congress, LC-USZ62-113600, Copyright by Standard Scenic Company: 52 (bottom); Library of Congress, LC-USZ62-116013: 53; Library of Congress, LC-USZ62-93510: 55 (top); Library of Congress Prints and Photographs Division, pan 6a33285: 59; Library of Congress, Prints and Photographs Division, LC-USZ62-26004: 60; Library of Congress Prints and Photographs Division, LC-USZ62-63740: 61; Library of Congress, New York World-Telegram and the Sun Newspaper Photograph Collection, LC-USZ62-132498: 64 (top); Library of Congress, New York World-Telegram and the Sun Newspaper Photograph Collection, LC-USZ62-115090: 67 (top right); Library of Congress, New York World-Telegram and the Sun Newspaper Photograph Collection, LC-USZ62-121957: 67 (bottom); Library of Congress, LC-USZ62-99614: 69 (bottom); Library of Congress, LC-USZ62-98013: 70 (bottom); Library of Congress Prints and Photographs Division, LC-USZ62-35222: 70 (top); Library of Congress Prints and Photographs Division, LC-USE6-D-008870: 73; Library of Congress Prints and Photographs Division, LC-USZ62-16555: 74 (top); Library of Congress, Prints and Photographs Division, LC-USZ62-128756: 75; Library of Congress, LC-USZ62-104727, USSTAF photo by Gaston & Morgan: 78 (bottom); Library of Congress, LC-USZ62-99393: 78 (top); Library of Congress, New York World-Telegram and the Sun Newspaper Photograph Collection, LC-USZ62-134192: 79; Library of Congress, New York World-Telegram & Sun Collection, LC-USZ62-111090: 81 (top); Library of Congress, Prints and Photographs Division, LC-USZ62-126589: 84 (top); Library of Congress, New York World-Telegram and the Sun Newspaper Photograph Collection, LC-USZ62-128857: 86

PICTURE SOURCES

Montana Historical Society: 15 (top); 19 (top and bottom); 20 (top, middle, and bottom); 26 (top and bottom); 30 (left and right); 31; 38; 41; 46; 48; 50 (top); 51 (bottom); 52 (top); 62; 64 (bottom); 65 (bottom); 74 (bottom); 80; 81 (bottom); 82 (top); 87

Norma Smith Papers, Collection 2329, **Montana State University Libraries**: 82 (bottom); 83; 84 (bottom)

The Schlesinger Library, Radcliffe Institute, Harvard University: Front cover; 42 (top and bottom); 51 (top); 67 (top left); 76; 77; 89; Back cover

Jane Addams Collection, **Swarthmore College Peace Collection**: 24 (top and bottom); Swarthmore College Peace Collection: 55 (bottom); Records of the Women's International League for Peace and Freedom, Swarthmore College Peace Collection: 58; Martha Fruend-Hoppe Collection, Swarthmore College Peace Collection: 66; Records of the National Council for Prevention of War, Swarthmore College Peace Collection: 69 (top)

The University of Montana–Missoula: Missoula River, 1925, Mss 249, R.H. McKay Collection, K. Ross Toole Archives, The University of Montana–Missoula: 14; Missoula, Front Street Looking East, ca. 1889, Mss 249, R.H. McKay Collection, K. Ross Toole Archives, The University of Montana–Missoula: 15 (bottom); Flathead Indian Women on horseback, undated, Mss 486, Morton J. Elrod Papers, K. Ross Toole Archives, The University of Montana–Missoula: 18; Horse Car Days in Missoula, undated, Mss 249, R.H. McKay Collection, K. Ross Toole Archives, The University of Montana–Missoula: 21; Menu, undated, Montana Pamphlet Collection, K. Ross Toole Archives, The University of Montana–Missoula: 37 (top right); Jeannette Rankin Letter to Constituent, June 1, 1917, Mss 139, Jeannette Rankin Papers, K. Ross Toole Archives, The University of Montana–Missoula: 50 (bottom); Campaign Button, "Jeannette Rankin for Congress," 1940, Mss 139, Jeannette Rankin Papers, K. Ross Toole Archives, The University of Montana–Missoula: 72

Washington State Historical Society, Tacoma: 27; 28; 29 (bottom left and right)

Woman's Home Companion: 63; 65 (top)

INDEX

Italicized page numbers refer to illustrations.

A
Addams, Jane, 24, *24, 28, 58,* 58–59
American Civil Liberties Union, 77
American Legion, 68, *68*
Anaconda Copper Mining Company, 43, 44, *52,* 52–53
Anthony, Katharine, *63, 65*

B
Boston, Massachusetts, 22–23
Boys' club, 64
Brenau College, 68, *68*
Bureau of Printing and Engraving, *53,* 53–54

C
Catt, Carrie Chapman, 36, *36,* 41, 46, 49–51
Chicago peace parades, 67
Churchill, Winston, 77
Cold War, 84, *84*
Columbia University School of Social Work, 24
Congressional Union, 48, *48*
Coolidge, Calvin, 62

E
Emporia Gazette, 76
Eugene Daily News, 76

F
France, *59,* 59–60, *60*
Franco, Francisco, 70

G
Gandhi, Mahatma, 81, *81*
Georgia Peace Society, 65
Gilder, Jeannette, 33
"Grab Act," 79
Great Depression, 67, *67*–68, 70
Gulf of Tonkin Resolution, 85

H
Heterodoxy Club, 32, 62–63
Hitler, Adolph, 61, 69, *69*–70, 79
Hodges, Bobbie, 87
Hull House, 24, *24*

I
Indians
  Chief Joseph, 17
  Nez Perce Indians, 17
  nonviolent attitudes toward, 66
  Salish Indians, 18, *18*
  treatment of by U.S. Army, 15, 17–19

J
Japan, 70, *70,* 74, *74,* 75, *75,* 78, 79, *79,* 80
Jeannette Rankin Brigade, *11,* 11–12, 87, *88*
Johnson, Lyndon, 85

K
Kennedy, John F., 77–78, *84*
Khrushchev, Nikita, *84*
King, Coretta Scott, 87
King, Martin Luther, Jr., 81, 84, 87
Kitchin, Claude, 49

L
Ladies' Home Journal, The, Feb. 1915, editorial, *57*
LaGuardia, Fiorello, *63, 64,* 77
Lend-Lease Act, 73, *73*
Libby, Frederick, *69,* 69–70
Liberty Loan Bonds, 53–54, *55,* 55–56

M
Macon Evening News, 69
Mansfield, Senator Mike, 87, *87*
Maternity and Infancy Care Act, 62
McCall's Magazine, 77
Military buildup
  Europe, 73

INDEX

in Germany, 59–61, *70*, 70–71
in Italy, 70, 71
in the U.S., 44, 70, 71, *84*
Japan, *70*, 78, 79
Vietnam, 84–85
Montana
    background of Jeannette Rankin, 12,
        14–21
    colleges, 20, *20*, *84*
    congressmen, 44
    Missoula, *14, 15*, 16, 17, *21*, 26, *26*, *31*
    Montana State University, 20, *20*, 25
    state capitol, *30*, 30–31
    statehood, 15
    suffrage movement, 30–31, *31, 35*, 35–38,
        37, 38
Mussolini, Benito, *69*, 79

N

National American Woman Suffrage
    Association (NAWSA), 33, 36, 46, 50
National Consumers' League, 62
National Council for the Prevention of
    War, 69, *69*
Nazi Party, 61, 69–70, 78, 79
Nehru, Jawaharlal, 81, *81*
Neutrality Acts, 66, 71
New Deal, 70
New Women, 32
New York City, 22, 23, *23*, 24–25, *25*,
    32–33, 67
New York School of Philanthropy, 24–25,
    25
New York State, 32, 35–36
New York Women's Suffrage Party, 32
New Zealand, *40*, 40–41
Nuclear weapons, 79
    atomic bombs dropped on Japan, 79, *79*
    Soviet Union, 84, *84*
    United States, 84, *84*
Nye, Senator Gerald, 66, *66*

P

Parkman, Francis, 33
Paul, Alice, 49
Peace movement
    1916 campaign, 43–44
    aftermath of World War I, 59–60, 61
    Committee for a Sane Nuclear Policy, 84
    International Congress of Women, 60–61
    National Council for the Prevention of
        War, 69, *69*
    Neutrality Acts, 66, 71
    peace messages, 66–67
    Vietnam War, 12, 84–88
    voting against World War I, *48–53*,
        48–57, *55, 57*
    Women's International League for Peace
        and Freedom (WILPF), *58*, 58–61
    World War II, 73–78
Plate-Printer, 54
Progressive reform movement, 23–24, 26,
    66

R

Rankin, Dorothy (niece), 62, 64, *87*
Rankin, Edna (sister), 15, *19*, 21, 25, 34,
    35, 42, 64, *64*, 80, *87*
Rankin, Grace (sister), 15, *19*, 21, 25, 42,
    64, 80
Rankin, Harriet (sister), 15, *15, 19*, 25, 42,
    52, *64*
Rankin, Jeannette
    1916 campaign, *41*, 41–47, *42, 43, 44, 46*
    1918 campaign, 56–57
    1940 campaign, 72, 72–73
    appearance, 11, *11, 19, 19*, 25, *26, 30*, 45,
        51, 58, 65, 74, 81
    The Buds, *20*
    childhood, 12, 14–18, 89
    college education, 20, *20*, 24–25, *25*, 27,
        68, 84, 85
    as congressperson, 13, 46–57, 72, 72–79,
        89

INDEX

farm in Georgia, *62*, 62–65, 80, 82, *82*, *83*

Honorary Degree of Doctor of Laws, *84*, *85*

letters to constituents, *50*

political cartoon, *51*

as suffragist, 27–29, *30*, 30–39, 89

travels after Congressional term, *81*, 81–83

travels to Egypt, *82*

travels to Europe, 58, *58*, 70, 71

travels to France, 59–60, *59–60*

travels to India, 81, 82

travels to Japan, *81*

travels to New Zealand, *40*, 40–41

Rankin, John (father), *14*, *15*, 16–19, *19*, 21, 31, 66

Rankin, John (nephew), 64

Rankin, Mary (sister), 15, *19*, 25, 42, *64*

Rankin, Olive (Pickering) (mother), *15*, 16, *19*, 21, 51, 64, *64*, 79, 80, 82

Rankin, Philena (sister), *15*, 19

Rankin, Wellington (brother), 15, *15*, *19*, 22, 25, *41*, 42, 44, 45, 50, 51, 64, *64*, *74*, *75*, *80*, 82

Rayburn, Sam, 74

Republican Party, 42–43, 56

Robinson family, 82, *83*

Roosevelt, Eleanor, 33, 67

Roosevelt, Franklin D., 33, 67, 70, 71, 73, *74*, *75*

Roosevelt, Theodore, 22, 23, 28, 42–43

S
San Francisco, California, 23, 24

Seattle, Washington, 27–28

Second International Congress of Women for Permanent Peace, 58, *58*–61

Settlement houses, 24

Slayden, Ellen Maury, 48

Snowdon, Ethel, 60

Social work, 23–27, *61*, 62

Spokane, Washington, 26

Stout, Tom, 37

Suffrage, women's

cartoons, *29*, 37

constitutional amendment, 33, 54–55, 61

flyers, *27*, 27–28, *28*, 37

in Montana, 30–31, *31*, 35, 35–38, *37*, *38*

New York Women's Suffrage Party, 32

passage of, 61

song, 38

suffragists and World War I, 48–51

timeline, 39

Washington State, *27*, 27–29

Sunshine Club, 64–65

Susan B. Anthony Hall of Fame, 88, 89

T
Telegraph Hill Neighborhood Association, 24

Tennyson, "The Charge of the Light Brigade," 20

Timeline, 90–92

U
U.S. Congress

1916 campaign, *41*, 41–47, *42*, *43*, *44*, *46*

1918 campaign, 56–57

1940 campaign, 72, *72*–73

House of Representatives, 45, 48, 49, *49*, *50*, 52

U.S. Constitution, 27, 33, 54–55, 61

U.S. Supreme Court, 83

University of Washington, 27

V
Vietnam Veterans Against the War, 86

Vietnam War

antiwar protests, 11, 12, 84–88

impact on Vietnamese civilians, *86*

military buildup, 84–85

INDEX

W

Washington, D.C. *See also* U.S. Congress
  1905 Inaugural Ball, *22*, *22*–*23*
  1932 peace march, 67
  Bureau of Printing and Engraving, *53*,
    53–54
  Jeannette Rankin Brigade, *11*, 11–12, 87,
    88
  Jeannette Rankin's apartment, 51–52
  suffrage movement, 32–33
  suffrage parade in, 33–34, *34*, *35*
Wilson, Woodrow, *33*, 33–34, 44, 47, 49,
  49, 53, 60
Winestine, Belle, 52
Women's Home Companion, 62
Women's International League for Peace
  and Freedom (WILPF), *58*, 58–61
World War I
  aftermath, 58–61, *59*, *60*, 66, 75
  Europe aftermath, 59, *59*, 61
  France aftermath, 59, *59*, 60, *60*
  hardships of, 56
  Liberty Loan Bonds, *55*, 55–56
  opposition to, 47, 49–50, 75
  overview of, 47
  trenches, *55*
  United States entry into, 43–44, 47, 49
World War II
  atomic bombs dropped on Japan, 79, *79*
  end of, 79, 80
  Europe aftermath, 78
  Japanese takeover of China, *70*, 79
  military buildup in Europe, 73
  military buildup in Germany, 59–61, *70*,
    70–71
  military buildup in Japan, *70*, 78, 79
  nuclear weapons, *84*
  opposition to, 74–76, *76*, 78
  overview of, 79
  Pearl Harbor, 74, *74*, 79
  post-war prosperity, 84